AN ABC OF COLOR

For a complete free catalog
INTERNATIONAL PUBLISHERS
PO Box 3042, JAF Sta.
NY NY 10116
phone (212) 366-9816   fax -9820

website:
www.intpubnyc.com

AN ABC OF COLOR
BY W.E.B. DU BOIS

Selections
chosen by the author
from
over a half century
of his writings

With an Introduction by
John Oliver Killens

International Publishers
New York

First published by Seven Seas Books, Berlin, 1963.
International Publishers editions in association
  with Seven Seas Books, 1969, 1971, 1983.

This International Publishers edition by arrangement
with Kraus International Publications, a division of
Kraus Organization, Ltd.

This printing 2001

Printed in the United States of America

.

Front cover drawing by Oliver Harrington

Briefly,
ABOUT THE AUTHOR

William Edward Burghardt Du Bois was
born three years after the end of the
American Civil War on February 23 1868 in
Great Barrington, Massachusetts. He was
the great-grandson of an African slave
who gained his freedom as a soldier
in the American Revolution. Other ancestors were of French and Dutch origin. On
August 27 1963, on the eve of the March
on Washington, death came to the man who
has been called "the father" of the black
liberation and the Pan-African movements.
He was in his ninety-sixth year. Academi-
cians on every continent paid homage to
him. And countless peoples, who long for
and fight for peace everywhere on this
earth, mourned the man who had been given
a Lenin Peace Prize — for peace was his
life's work. Millions of black Americans
and Africans who knew and revered him
paid fervent homage. Dr. Du Bois was indeed an exceptional man and this book, in
which he selected from sixty years of his
writings is indeed an exceptional book.

CONTENTS

AN INTRODUCTION

It was early morning of the March on Washington. We stood in the busy lobby of the Willard Hotel. I believe there were among those with me, chatting quietly, excitedly, nervously, James Baldwin and Sidney Poitier. Outside, Washington, D.C. was like an occupied city, with police and helmeted soldiers everywhere. There were very few civilians on the streets that memorable morning. By air, busses, automobiles, on foot, people were gathering on the outskirts of the city by the tens of thousands. The downtown government district was hushed and awesomely white as only Washington can be. Our group was waiting for transportation to the National Airport, where we were to participate in a press conference before the March began.

Some one walked over to our group and said, "The old man died." Just that. And not one of us asked, "What old man?" We all knew who the old man was, because he was our old man. He belonged to every one of us. And we belonged to him. To some of us he was our patron saint, our teacher and our major prophet. He was Big Daddy? No. He was Big Grand Daddy. More than any other single human being, he, through the sheer power of his vast and profound intelligence, his tireless scholarship and his fierce dedication to the cause of black liberation, had brought us and the other two hundred and fifty thousand souls to this place, to this moment in time and space. In the small group there in the Willard lobby, we all wore solemn faces now, but there was no weeping amongst us on that historic summer morning. A sense of tremendous loss, yes, profoundly felt. But there was this other thing we shared, a feeling of dignity and pride in the knowledge of a life well spent, well lived, a life of quality as

9

well as quantity, an unusual combination. He was an unusual man.

We felt, "Well done, thou great and faithful servant." For he had spent a lifetime in the service of humankind. There was here a kind of poetic finale that made sense to us, that he should die on the very eve of this historic occasion. He was a man of irony. He had run a tremendous race, and now it would be up to us, all of us everywhere, to take the torch and carry it forward. He had left us a legacy, of scholarship and struggle. And this was the kind of monument we promised ourselves we would build in his name, a monument of struggle. It was also a bit of poetic justice that he died in a place he loved so dearly, Mother Africa, the land of his forefathers, he, the father of Pan-Africanism.

And now, it is a great thing that Du Bois's *An ABC of Color* is being republished. It is a book that contains so much of his genius, his vast wisdom, his tremendous wit and humor. The world desperately needs this book. Especially black Americans need this book now as never before, as the confrontations between blacks and the white establishment mount almost hourly. Actually we need the republication of all of his books. So many young Americans do not know of men like Paul Robeson and Du Bois. So many think that the militant black movement in the U.S.A. began two years ago (six months even), which is to say, the very day the hour they joined the movement, and not a single moment earlier.

Here is a book which will provide for them and for all of us an historical perspective. Here we have selections from over a half of a century of the writings of W.E.B. Du Bois. But more than that, here we have the perceptions of almost a century of living, living up to the hilt of man's capacity to live.

At the beginning of the twentieth century, Dr. Du Bois put the Western World on notice that the problem of the twentieth century was the problem of the color line, the relationship of the Western World with the peoples of color in Africa and Asia and the islands of the seas. Years later, he wrote, with even greater certainty: *Most men in the world are colored. A belief in humanity means a belief in colored men. The future world will, in all reasonable possibility, be what colored men make it.* In 1955, the Pan-Africanist George Padmore wrote, in comment on the Du Bois prophecy: *This is the inescapable challenge of the second part of the twentieth century.*

Yes, Dr. Du Bois was a major prophet, but who would listen to a black prophet in that far-off era of good feelings in the grand old days of endless frontier and glorious empire, when Western man thought that he would rule the roost forever, or, at the very least, for another thousand years? It was a time of Uncle Tom and Aunt Jemima and good old Gunga Din. It was the day of the "kindly missionary" and the "noble savage," when situations and relationships had been arranged forever, ordained divinely by the Gods. Notwithstanding, the prophecy of the major prophet has come to pass. Observe how the world has changed since the Second World Wide Madness. Take notice of the United Nations, that organization which began as a Gentlemen's Agreement, an exclusive club of Great White Fathers, paternalistic trustees of three quarters of humanity. Look at the world today and recall the words of the Last of the Great Anglo-Saxons, Winston Churchill, who proclaimed to one and all, that he had not taken over the reins of Her Britannic Majesty's Government to administer over the dissolution of the British Empire. Recall that little island's arrogant boast, that the sun never set on the British Empire. But the sunset and Sir Winston notwithstanding, the Empire has dissolved, is dissolving.

In *ABC of Color*, we learn of the first Pan-African Congress, held in London in 1900, called by Henry Sylvester-Williams, a Trinidadian, and attended by the young Du Bois. The Congress elected Du Bois Chairman of the Committee on Address. His address "To the Nations of the World," is contained in this volume. Thus it was that the word "Pan-Africanism" became a part of the universal language, and the concept, itself, became a rallying point for the African liberation movement. That Congress in 1900 gave birth to the concept, but it was Du Bois, more than any other, who nurtured the baby and raised it to maturity. Thus it can be truthfully said that W.E.B. Du Bois was the father of Pan-Africanism.

World-changing is a hazardous pursuit. The lives of men who would dare to change the world and challenge the Gods of Power and the Status Quo are never smooth, indeed are always fraught with great danger. Such was the life of the author of *An ABC of Color*. He was the greatest American intellectual of the twentieth century, did his undergraduate work at Fisk University in Nashville, Tennessee, studied at Harvard University and the University of Berlin. He held degrees of Doctor of Philosophy, Doctor of Laws, Doctor of Literature, Doctor of Humanities and Doctor of Historical Science. Obviously he was eminently prepared to "climb the ladder to success"t and assume the role of hero in the Great American Success Story, and win for himself fame and wealth and respectability, except for two considerations. One: He was a black American. Two: He was a freedom fighter, who would not compromise with tyranny. He might have won the plaudits and the lucrative blandishments of the Power Structure had he chosen to play the game. But, instead of playing the game, he chose to spend a lifetime dedicated to exposing the game. And there is the rub. That is why at the age of eighty-three he found himself in handcuffs and treated like a common criminal in Washington, D.C. Some black men who knew him well did not come to his assistance, did not stand up and say, "I know this man. He has always fought for justice and for righteousness." Many black folk who owed him so much failed him at this hour. Some were too busy scurrying for cover, only to find out ultimately that there really was no hiding place down here, nor is there now, nor will there ever be. There is much the black movement can learn from this experience. Essentially the lesson here is, that we black folk must choose our own spokesmen and our own leaders, if we are serious about the business of black liberation. We black folk must never again turn our backs on our leaders just because the Establishment attacks them. A leader of the oppressed becomes suspect to his people when the oppressors take him to their bosoms. We need to remember this lesson, because the attacks against black leadership are going to multiply as the conflict increases in intensity. Witness what happened to the Three M's, Brothers Medgar, Malcolm and Martin.

Du Bois was a founder of the Niagara Movement and the National Association for the Advancement of Colored People. He was also founder of *The Crisis* magazine. Many of the articles appearing in the early *Crisis* are contained in *An ABC of Color*. This book is rich with perceptions and insights and experiences of a magnificent life. There is tragedy here as well as irony and humor. Aside from all that, Du Bois had a tremendous command of language — word power. One could read this book for the sheer beauty of the language

In the struggle mounting throughout the world today between the haves and have-nots, there is much to be gained from the writings of Dr. Du Bois, a man who, during his entire adult life, always stood in the forefront of the struggle. No single human being contributed more to our understanding of colonialism and the anatomy of white racism than W.E.B. Du Bois. I hope this new edition of *An ABC of Color* gets the audience it so richly deserves. We desperately need Du Bois's sharp, profound perceptions in the now-days and in the turbulent days that lie ahead.

September, 1968
New York City   JOHN OLIVER KILLENS

THE END OF AN ERA

1896—1900 ... For thirty-five years, the
scientific study of a social problem was
Dr. Du Bois' main pursuit. This was the
study of the background of inequality visited upon Americans of African descent.
His research spanned a period which dated
back to the days of slavery and continued
through the time when the Negro became a
freed man. Dr. Du Bois began publishing
papers on this subject at the end of the
nineteenth century.... The following section contains excerpts from this period.

SLAVES IN THE UNITED STATES

The first published work of Dr. Du Bois appeared in 1896 as the first volume of the Harvard University Historical Series. It was entitled The Suppression of the African Slave Trade to the United States of America, 1638—1870. *It had been originally written as his doctoral thesis. This extract shows how America made slaves of Du Bois' ancestors.*

Here was a rich new land, the wealth of which was to be had in return for ordinary manual labor. Had the country been conceived of as existing primarily for the benefit of its actual inhabitants, it might have waited for natural increase or immigration to supply the needed hands; but both Europe and the earlier colonists themselves regarded this land as existing chiefly for the benefit of Europe, and as designed to be exploited, as rapidly and ruthlessly as possible, of the boundless wealth of its resources. This was the primary excuse for the rise of the African slave trade to America.

Every experiment of such a kind, however, where the moral standard of a people is lowered for the sake of a material advantage, is dangerous in just such proportion as that advantage is great. In this case it was great. For at least a century, in the West Indies and the southern United States, agriculture flourished, trade increased, and English manufactures were nourished, in just such proportion as Americans stole Negroes and worked them to death. This advantage, to be sure, became much smaller in later times, and at one critical period was, at least in the Southern States, almost *nil*; but energetic efforts were wanting, and, before the nation was aware, slavery had seized a new and well-nigh immovable footing in the Cotton Kingdom.

The colonists averred with perfect truth that they did

not commence this fatal traffic, but that it was imposed upon them from without. Nevertheless, all too soon did they lay aside scruples against it and hasten to share its material benefits. Even those who braved the rough Atlantic for the highest moral motives fell early victims to the allurements of this system. Thus, throughout colonial history, in spite of many honest attempts to stop the further pursuit of the slave trade, we notice back of nearly all such attempts a certain moral apathy, an indisposition to attack the evil with the sharp weapons which its nature demanded. Consequently, there developed steadily, irresistibly, a vast social problem, which required two centuries and a half for a nation of trained European stock and boasted moral fibre to solve.

Excerpt: *The Suppression of the African Slave Trade*, 1896

CREDO

At the advent of the twentieth century, Du Bois was thirty-three years of age and teaching and carrying on research at Atlanta University, a Negro institution in Georgia. Among the author's first publications was a Credo, written in 1900, in which he tried to reconcile his religious belief with the ethics of the race problem.

I believe in God, who made of one blood all nations that on earth do dwell. I believe that all men, black and brown and white, are brothers, varying through time and opportunity, in form and gift and feature, but differing in no essential particular, and alike in soul and the possibility of infinite development.

Especially do I believe in the Negro Race: in the beauty of its genius, the sweetness of its soul, and its strength in

17

that meekness which shall yet inherit this turbulent earth.

I believe in Pride of race and lineage and self: in pride of self so deep as to scorn injustice to other selves; in pride of lineage so great as to despise no man's father; in pride of race so chivalrous as neither to offer bastardy to the weak nor beg wedlock of the strong, knowing that men may be brothers in Christ, even though they be not brothers in law.

I believe in Service — humble, reverent service, from the blackening of boots to the whitening of souls; for Work is Heaven, Idleness Hell, and Wage is the "Well done!" of the Master, who summoned all them that labor and are heavy laden, making no distinction between the black, sweating cotton hands of Georgia and the first families of Virginia, since all distinction not based on deed is devilish and not divine.

I believe in the Devil and his angels, who wantonly work to narrow the opportunity of struggling human beings, especially if they be black; who spit in the faces of the fallen, strike them that cannot strike again, believe the worst and work to prove it, hating the image which their Maker stamped on a brother's soul.

I believe in the Prince of Peace. I believe that War is Murder. I believe that armies and navies are at bottom the tinsel and braggadocio of oppression and wrong, and I believe that the wicked conquest of weaker and darker nations by nations whiter and stronger but foreshadows the death of that strength.

I believe in Liberty for all men: the space to stretch their arms and their souls, the right to breathe and the right to vote, the freedom to choose their friends, enjoy the sunshine, and ride on the railroads, uncursed by color; thinking, dreaming, working as they will in a kingdom of beauty and love.

I believe in the Training of Children, black even as white; the leading out of little souls into the green pastures and beside the still waters, not for self nor peace, but for life lit by some large vision of beauty and goodness and truth; lest we forget, and the sons of the fathers, like Esau, for mere meat barter their birthright in a mighty nation.

Finally, I believe in Patience — patience with the weakness of the Weak and the strength of the Strong, the prejudice of the Ignorant and the ignorance of the Blind; patience with the tardy triumph of Joy and the mad chastening of Sorrow; patience with God!

Excerpt: DARKWATER (N.Y., Harcourt, Brace & World, Inc., 1920)

TO THE NATIONS OF THE WORLD

The idea of Pan-Africanism first arose as a manifestation of fraternal solidarity among Africans and peoples of African descent. It was originally conceived by a West Indian barrister, Mr. Henry Sylvester-Williams* of Trinidad, who practised at the English bar at the end of the nineteenth century and beginning of the present. It appears that during his undergraduate days and after, Mr. Sylvester-Williams established close association with West Africans in Britain and later acted as legal adviser to several African chiefs and other native dignitaries who visited the United Kingdom on political missions to the Colonial Office.

To combat the aggressive policies of British imperialists Mr. Sylvester-Williams took the initiative in convening

---

* Henry Sylvester-Williams, born 1868 in Trinidad, was an elementary school teacher who later studied and practised law in England. He travelled extensively in South Africa, the United States and Canada. He returned to Trinidad where he was admitted to the Bar. He died in Port of Spain on March 26, 1911.

a Pan-African conference in London in 1900 as a forum of protest against the aggression of white colonizers and, at the same time, to make an appeal to the missionary and abolitionist traditions of the British people to protect the Africans from the depredations of the Empire builders. This meeting attracted attention, put the word "Pan-Africanism" in the dictionaries for the first time, and had some thirty delegates mainly from England and the West Indies, with a few colored North Americans. The conference was welcomed by the Lord Bishop of London and a promise was obtained from Queen Victoria, through Joseph Chamberlain,* not to "overlook the interest and welfare of the native races." Unfortunately, Mr. Sylvester-Williams returned to the West Indies some years later and died. The Pan-African concept remained dormant until it was revived by Dr. Du Bois after the First World War. Thanks to his devotion and sacrifice, he gave body and soul to Sylvester-Williams' "original idea of Pan-Africanism and broadened its perspective."**

Dr. Du Bois attended the Pan-African Conference in London in 1900 and was made Chairman of the Resolutions Committee and wrote the Address which follows.

In the metropolis of the modern world, in this the closing year of the nineteenth century, there has been assembled a congress of men and women of African blood, to deliberate solemnly upon the present situation and outlook of the darker races of mankind. The problem of the twentieth century is the problem of the color-line, the question as to how far differences of race — which show themselves chiefly in the color of the skin and the texture of the hair — will hereafter be made the basis of denying to over half the world the right of sharing to their utmost ability the opportunities and privileges of modern civilization.

* Joseph Chamberlain (1836—1914): British statesman
** Padmore: *Pan-Africanism or Communism*

To be sure, the darker races are today the least advanced in culture according to European standards. This has not, however, always been the case in the past, and certainly the world's history, both ancient and modern, has given many instances of no despicable ability and capacity among the blackest races of men.

In any case, the modern world must remember that in this age when the ends of the world are being brought so near together the millions of black men in Africa, America, and the Islands of the Sea, not to speak of the brown and yellow myriads elsewhere, are bound to have a great influence upon the world in the future, by reason of sheer numbers and physical contact. If now the world of culture bends itself towards giving Negroes and other dark men the largest and broadest opportunity for education and self-development, then this contact and influence is bound to have a beneficial effect upon the world and hasten human progress. But if, by reason of carelessness, prejudice, greed and injustice, the black world is to be exploited and ravished and degraded, the results must be deplorable, if not fatal — not simply to them, but to the high ideals of justice, freedom and culture which a thousand years of Christian civilization have held before Europe.

And now, therefore, to these ideals of civilization, to the broader humanity of the followers of the Prince of Peace, we, the men and women of Africa in world congress assembled, do now solemnly appeal:

Let the world take no backward step in that slow but sure progress which has successively refused to let the spirit of class, of caste, of privilege, or of birth, debar from life, liberty and the pursuit of happiness a striving human soul.

Let not color or race be a feature of distinction between white and black men, regardless of worth or ability.

Let not the natives of Africa be sacrificed to the greed of gold, their liberties taken away, their family life debauched, their just aspirations repressed, and avenues of advancement and culture taken from them.

Let not the cloak of Christian missionary enterprise be allowed in the future, as so often in the past, to hide the ruthless economic exploitation and political downfall of less developed nations, whose chief fault has been reliance on the plighted faith of the Christian church.

Let the British nation, the first modern champion of Negro freedom, hasten to crown the work of Wilberforce, and Clarkson, and Buxton, and Sharpe, Bishop Colenso, and Livingstone, and give, as soon as practicable, the rights of responsible government to the black colonies of Africa and the West Indies.

Let not the spirit of Garrison,* Phillips, and Douglass wholly die out in America; may the conscience of a great nation rise and rebuke all dishonesty and unrighteous oppression toward the American Negro, and grant to him the right of franchise, security of person and property, and generous recognition of the great work he has accomplished in a generation toward raising nine millions of human beings from slavery to manhood.

Let the German Empire, and the French Republic, true to their great past, remember that the true worth of colonies lies in their prosperity and progress, and that justice, impartial alike to black and white, is the first element of prosperity.

* William Lloyd Garrison, Wendell Phillips, Frederick Douglass: Famous abolitionists and orators

Let the Congo Free State become a great central Negro State of the world, and let its prosperity be counted not simply in cash and commerce, but in the happiness and true advancement of its black people.

Let the nations of the World respect the integrity and independence of the free Negro States of Abyssinia, Liberia, Haiti, and the rest, and let the inhabitants of these States, the independent tribes of Africa, the Negroes of the West Indies and America, and the black subjects of all nations take courage, strive ceaselessly, and fight bravely, that they may prove to the world their incontestible right to be counted among the great brotherhood of mankind.

Thus we appeal with boldness and confidence to the Great Powers of the civilized world, trusting in the wide spirit of humanity, and the deep sense of justice of our age, for a generous recognition of the righteousness of our cause.

ALEXANDER WALTERS (Bishop)
President Pan-African Association

HENRY B. BROWN
Vice-President

H. SYLVESTER-WILLIAMS
General Secretary

W. E. BURGHARDT DU BOIS
Chairman Committee on Address

Address: *To the Nations of the World,* 1900

THE NEW CENTURY

1903—1909 ... The early years of the new
century were for Dr. Du Bois years of accomplishment, years of study, of political activity — and of personal tragedy ...
It was the time when American Negroes began to form their own organizations which
would combat discrimination. Dr. Du Bois
was a spokesman for this new movement. He
expressed for Black America these new aspirations ... The excerpts which appear in
this section throw light upon the time ...

OF THE PASSING OF THE FIRST-BORN

In 1903, Dr. Du.Bois published a book of essays, called
Souls of Black Folk. *It was his most popular book and
went through twenty-eight editions. It had wide influence
on American thought concerning Negroes. The chapter on
the death of his first child is here reproduced.*

Unto you a child is born," sang the bit of yellow paper
that fluttered into my room one brown October morning.
Then the fear of fatherhood mingled wildly with the joy
of creation; I wondered how it looked and how it felt —
what were its eyes, and how its hair curled and crumpled
itself. And I thought in awe of her, she who had slept with
Death to tear a man-child from underneath her heart,
while I was unconsciously wandering. I fled to my wife
and child, repeating the while to myself half wonderingly,
"Wife and child? Wife and child?" — fled fast and faster
than boat and steam-car, and yet must ever impatiently
await them; away from the hard-voiced city, away from
the flickering sea into my own Berkshire Hills that sit all
sadly guarding the gates of Massachusetts.

Up the stairs I ran to the wan mother and whimpering
babe, to the sanctuary on whose altar a life at my bidding
had offered itself to win a life, and won. What is this
tiny formless thing, this newborn wail from an unknown
world, all head and voice? I handle it curiously, and watch
perplexed its winking, breathing, and sneezing. I did not
love it then; it seemed a ludicrous thing to love; but her
I loved, my girl-mother, she whom now I saw unfolding
like the glory of the morning — the transfigured woman.

Through her I came to love the wee thing, as it grew
and waxed strong; as its little soul unfolded itself in
twitter and cry and half-formed word, and as its eyes
caught the gleam and flash of life. How beautiful he was,
with his olive-tinted flesh and dark gold ringlets, his

eyes of mingled blue and brown, his perfect little limbs, and the soft voluptuous roll which the blood of Africa had moulded into his features! I held him in my arms, after we had sped far away to our Southern home — held him, and glanced at the hot red soil of Georgia and the breathless city of a hundred hills, and felt a vague unrest. Why was his hair tinted with gold? An evil omen was golden hair in my life. Why had not the brown of his eyes crushed out and killed the blue? for brown were his father's eyes, and his father's father's. And thus in the Land of the Color-line I saw, as it fell across my baby, the shadow of the Veil.

Within the Veil was he born, said I; and there within shall he live, a Negro and a Negro's son. Holding in that little head — ah, bitterly! — the unbowed pride of a hunted race, clinging with that tiny dimpled hand — ah, wearily! — to a hope not hopeless but unhopeful, and seeing with those bright wondering eyes that peer into my soul a land whose freedom is to us a mockery and whose liberty a lie. I saw the shadow of the Veil as it passed over my baby, I saw the cold city towering above the blood-red land. I held my face beside his little cheek, showed him the star-children and the twinkling lights as they began to flash, and stilled with an evensong the unvoiced terror of my life.

So sturdy and masterful he grew, so filled with bubbling life, so tremulous with the unspoken wisdom of a life but eighteen months distant from the All-life — we were not far from worshipping this revelation of the divine, my wife and I. Her own life builded and moulded itself upon the child; he tinged her every dream and idealized her every effort. No hands but hers must touch and garnish those little limbs; no dress or frill must touch them that had not wearied her fingers; no voice but hers could coax him off to Dreamland, and she and he together spoke some soft and unknown tongue and in it held communion. I too mused above his little white bed; saw the strength of my own arm stretched onward through the ages through the newer strength of his; saw the dream of my black fathers stagger a step onward in the wild phantasm of the world; heard in his baby voice the voice of the Prophet that was to rise within the Veil.

And so we dreamed and loved and planned by fall and winter, and the full flush of the long Southern spring, till the hot winds rolled from the fetid Gulf, till the roses shivered and the still stern sun quivered its awful light over the hills of Atlanta. And then one night the little feet pattered wearily to the wee white bed, and the tiny hands trembled; and a warm flushed face tossed on the pillow, and we knew baby was sick. Ten days he lay there — a swift week and three endless days, wasting, wasting away. Cheerily the mother nursed him the first days, and laughed into the little eyes that smiled again. Tenderly then she hovered round him, till the smile fled away and Fear crouched beside the little bed.

Then the day ended not, and night was a dreamless terror, and joy and sleep slipped away. I hear now that Voice at midnight calling me from dull and dreamless trance, crying, "The Shadow of Death! The Shadow of Death!" Out into the starlight I crept, to rouse the gray physician — the Shadow of Death, the Shadow of Death. The hours trembled on; the night listened; the ghastly dawn glided like a tired thing across the lamplight. Then we two alone looked upon the child as he turned toward us with great eyes, and stretched his stringlike hands — the Shadow of Death! And we spoke no word, and turned away.

He died at eventide, when the sun lay like a brooding sorrow above the western hills, veiling its face; when the winds spoke not, and the trees, the great green trees he loved, stood motionless. I saw his breath beat quicker and quicker, pause, and then his little soul leapt like a star that travels in the night and left a world of darkness in its train. The day changed not; the same tall trees peeped in at the windows, the same green grass glinted in the setting sun. Only in the chamber of death writhed the world's most piteous thing — a childless mother.

I shirk not. I long for work. I pant for a life full of striving. I am no coward, to shrink before the rugged rush of the storm, nor even quail before the awful shadow of the Veil. But hearken, O Death! Is not this my life hard enough, is not that dull land that stretches its sneering web about me cold enough, is not all the world beyond these four little walls pitiless enough, but that thou must needs enter here — thou, O Death? About my head the thundering storm beat like a heartless voice, and the crazy forest pulsed with the curses of the weak; but what cared I, within my home beside my wife and baby boy? Wast thou so jealous of one little coign of happiness that thou must needs enter there, thou, O Death?

A perfect life was his, all joy and love, with tears to make it brighter, sweet as a summer's day beside the Housatonic. The world loved him; the women kissed his curls, the men looked gravely into his wonderful eyes, and the children hovered and fluttered about him. I can see him now, changing like the sky from sparkling laughter to darkening frowns, and then to wondering thoughtfulness as he watched the world. He knew no color-line, poor dear — and the Veil, though it shadowed him, had not yet darkened half his sun. He loved the white matron, he loved his black nurse; and in his little world walked souls alone, uncolored and unclothed. I — yea, all men — are larger and purer by the infinite breadth of that one little life. She who in simple clearness of vision sees beyond the stars said when he had flown, "He will be happy There; he ever loved beautiful things." And I, far more ignorant, and blind by the web of mine own weaving, sit alone winding words and muttering, "If still he be, and he be There, and there be a There, let him be happy, O Fate!"

Blithe was the morning of his burial, with bird and

song and sweet-smelling flowers. The trees whispered to the grass, but the children sat with hushed faces. And yet it seemed a ghostly unreal day — the wraith of Life. We seemed to rumble down an unknown street behind a little white bundle of posies, with the shadow of a song in our ears.

The busy city dinned about us; they did not say much, those pale-faced hurrying men and women; they did not say much — they only glanced and said, "Niggers!"

We could not lay him in the ground there in Georgia, for the earth there is strangely red; so we bore him away to the northward, with his flowers and his little folded hands. In vain, in vain! for where, O God! beneath thy broad blue sky shall my dark baby rest in peace — where Reverence dwells, and Goodness, and a Freedom that is free?

All that day and all that night there sat an awful gladness in my heart, nay, blame me not if I see the world thus darkly through the Veil — and my soul whispers ever to me, saying, "Not dead, not dead, but escaped; not bond, but free." No bitter meanness now shall sicken his baby heart till it die a living death, no taunt shall madden his happy boyhood. Fool that I was to think or wish that this little soul should grow choked and deformed within the Veil! I might have known that yonder deep unworldly look that ever and anon floated past his eyes was peering far beyond this narrow Now. In the poise of his little curl-crowned head did there not sit all that wild pride of being which his father had hardly crushed in his own heart? For what, forsooth, shall a Negro want with pride amid the studied humiliations of fifty million fellows? Well sped, my boy, before the world had dubbed your ambition insolence, had held your ideals unattainable, and taught you to cringe and bow. Better far this nameless void that stops my life than a sea of sorrow for you.

Idle words; he might have borne his burden more bravely than we — aye, and found it lighter too, some day; for surely, surely this is not the end. Surely there shall yet dawn some mighty morning to lift the Veil and set the prisoned free. Not for me — I shall die in my bonds — but for fresh young souls who have not known the night and waken to the morning; a morning when men ask of the workman, not "Is he white?" but "Can he work?" When men ask artists, not "Are they black?" but "Do they know?" Some morning this may be, long, long years to come. But now there wails, on that dark shore within the Veil, the same deep voice, *Thou shalt forego!* And all have I foregone at that command, and with small complaint — all save that fair young form that lies so coldly wed with death in the nest I had builded.

If one must have gone, why not I? Why may I not rest me from this restlessness and sleep from this wide waking? Was not the world's alembic, Time, in his young hands, and is not my time waning? Are there so many workers in the vineyard that the fair promise of this little body could lightly be tossed away? The wretched of my race that line the alleys of the nation sit fatherless and unmothered; but Love sat beside his cradle, and in his ear Wisdom waited to speak.

Perhaps now he knows the All-love, and needs not to be wise. Sleep, then, child — sleep till I sleep and waken to a baby voice and the ceaseless patter of little feet — above the Veil.

Excerpt: THE SOULS OF BLACK FOLK, (Chicago, A. C. McClurg & Co., 1903)

THE NIAGARA MOVEMENT

In 1905, the author organized the Niagara Movement to agitate for Negro rights. It held its most important meeting at Harper's Ferry, August 15 to 19, 1906 "to com-

memorate the 100th birthday of John Brown and the
jubilee of the Battle of Osawatomie." The resolutions
written by Dr. Du Bois follow.*

The men of the Niagara Movement, coming from the
toil of the year's hard work, and pausing a moment from
the earning of their daily bread, turn toward the nation
and again ask in the name of ten million the privilege of
a hearing. In the past year the work of the Negro hater
has flourished in the land. Step by step the defenders of
the rights of American citizens have retreated. The work
of stealing the black man's ballot has progressed and the
fifty and more representatives of stolen votes still sit in
the nation's capital. Discrimination in travel and public
accommodation has so spread that some of our weaker
brethren are actually afraid to thunder against color discrimination as such and are simply whispering for
ordinary decencies.

Against this the Niagara Movement eternally protests.
We will not be satisfied to take one jot or tittle less than
our full manhood rights. We claim for ourselves every
single right that belongs to a freeborn American, political,
civil and social; and until we get these rights we will
never cease to protest and assail the ears of America.
The battle we wage is not for ourselves alone, but for all
true Americans. It is a fight for ideals, lest this, our common fatherland, false to its founding, become in truth the
land of the Thief and the home of the Slave — a by-word
and a hissing among the nations for its sounding preten-
sions and pitiful accomplishment.

Never before in the modern age has a great and civilized folk threatened to adopt so cowardly a creed in the
treatment of its fellow-citizens, born and bred on its soil.

* John Brown (1800—59): martyred abolitionist, leader of
Negro rebellion

Stripped of verbiage and subterfuge and in its naked nastiness, the new American creed says: fear to let black men even try to rise lest they become the equals of the white. And this is the land that professes to follow Jesus Christ. The blasphemy of such a course is only matched by its cowardice.

In detail our demands are clear and unequivocal.

First. We would vote; with the right to vote goes everything: freedom, manhood, the honor of your wives, the chastity of your daughters, the right to work, and the chance to rise; let no man listen to those who deny this.

We want full manhood suffrage, and we want it now, henceforth and forever.

Second. We want discrimination in public accommodation to cease. Separation in railway and street cars, based simply on race and color, is un-American, undemocratic, and silly. We protest against all such discrimination.

Third. We claim the right of freemen to walk, talk and be with them that wish to be with us. No man has the right to choose another man's friends, and to attempt to do so is an impudent interference with the most fundamental human privilege.

Fourth. We want the laws enforced against rich as well as poor; against Capitalist as well as Laborer; against white as well as black. We are not more lawless than the white race, we are more often arrested, convicted and mobbed. We want justice even for criminals and outlaws. We want the Constitution of the country enforced. We want Congress to take charge of the Congressional elections. We want the Fourteenth Amendment carried out to the letter and every State disfranchised in Congress which attempts to disfranchise its rightful voters. We want the Fifteenth Amendment enforced and no State allowed to base its franchise simply on color.

The failure of the Republican Party in Congress at the

session just closed to redeem its pledge of 1904 with reference to suffrage conditions at the South seems a plain, deliberate, and premeditated breach of promise, and stamps that party as guilty of obtaining votes under false pretense.

Fifth. We want our children educated. The school system in the country districts of the South is a disgrace and in few towns and cities are the Negro schools what they ought to be. We want the national government to step in and wipe out illiteracy in the South. Either the United States will destroy ignorance or ignorance will destroy the United States.

And when we call for education, we mean real education. We believe in work. We ourselves are workers, but work is not necessarily education. Education is the development of power and ideal. We want our children trained as intelligent human beings should be, and we will fight for all time against any proposal to educate black boys and girls simply as servants and underlings, or simply for the use of other people. They have a right to know, to think, to aspire.

These are some of the chief things which we want. How shall we get them? By voting where we may vote; by persistent, unceasing agitation; by hammering at the truth; by sacrifice and work.

We do not believe in violence, neither in the despised violence of the raid nor the lauded violence of the soldier, nor the barbarous violence of the mob; but we do believe in John Brown, in that incarnate spirit of justice, that hatred of a lie, that willingness to sacrifice money, reputation, and life itself on the altar of right. And here on the scene of John Brown's martyrdom, we reconsecrate ourselves, our honor, our property to the final emancipation of the race for whose freedom John Brown died.

Excerpt: *Resolutions Niagara Movement*, 1906

A LITANY AT ATLANTA

*In the autumn of 1906, shortly after the Niagara Move-
ment meeting at Harper's Ferry, a riot broke out in Atlanta,
Georgia. It arose from the successful effort of corporations
to turn Hoke Smith's exposure of their lawlessness into
an attack on Negroes which Smith himself led. They were
falsely accused of crimes and then attacked by mobs.
Many were killed and their property destroyed. The news
reached the author in Alabama where he had gone to
study. He rushed home to his wife and baby. The poem
which follows, written en route, expresses his anguish.*

O Silent God, Thou whose voice afar in mist and
mystery hath left our ears an-hungered in these fearful
days —
   Hear us, good Lord!
Listen to us, Thy children: our faces dark with doubt are
made a mockery in Thy Sanctuary. With uplifted hands
we front Thy Heaven, O God, crying:
   We beseech Thee to hear us, good Lord!
We are not better than our fellows, Lord; we are but
weak and human men. When our devils do deviltry, curse
Thou the doer and the deed — curse them as we curse
them, do to them all and more than ever they have done
to innocence and weakness, to womanhood and home.
   Have mercy upon us, miserable sinners!
And yet, whose is the deeper guilt? Who made these
devils? Who nursed them in crime and fed them on injustice? Who ravished and debauched their mothers and
their grandmothers? Who bought and sold their crime
and waxed fat and rich on public iniquity?
   Thou knowest, good God!
Is this Thy Justice, O Father, that guile be easier than
innocence and the innocent be crucified for the guilt of
the untouched guilty?

Justice, O Judge of men!

Wherefore do we pray? Is not the God of the Fathers dead? Have not seers seen in Heaven's halls Thine hearsed and lifeless form stark amidst the black and rolling smoke of sin, where all along bow bitter forms of endless dead?

Awake, Thou that sleepest!

Thou art not dead, but flown afar, up hills of endless light, through blazing corridors of suns, where worlds do swing of good and gentle men, of women strong and free — far from the cozenage, black hypocrisy, and chaste prostitution of this shameful speck of dust!

Turn again, O Lord; leave us not to perish in our sin!

From lust of body and lust of blood —

Great God, deliver us!

From lust of power and lust of gold —

Great God, deliver us!

From the leagued lying of despot and of brute —

Great God, deliver us!

A city lay in travail, God our Lord, and from her loins sprang twin Murder and black Hate. Red was the midnight; clang, crack, and cry of death and fury filled the air and trembled underneath the stars where church spires pointed silently to Thee. And all this was to sate the greed of greedy men who hide behind the veil of vengeance!

Bend us Thine ear, O Lord!

In the pale, still morning we looked upon the deed. We stopped our ears and held our leaping hands, but they — did they not wag their heads and leer and cry with bloody jaws: *Cease from Crime!* The word was mockery, for thus they train a hundred crimes while we do cure one.

Turn again our captivity, O Lord!

Behold this maimed and broken thing, dear God; it was an humble black man, who toiled and sweated to save a bit from the pittance paid him. They told him: *Work and Rise!* He worked. Did this man sin? Nay, but someone told how someone said another did — one whom he had never seen nor known. Yet for that man's crime this man lieth maimed and murdered, his wife naked to shame, his children to poverty and evil.

Hear us, O heavenly Father!

Doth not this justice of hell stink in Thy nostrils, O God? How long shall the mounting flood of innocent blood roar in Thine ears and pound in our hearts for vengeance? Pile the pale frenzy of blood-crazed brutes, who do such deeds, high on Thine Altar, Jehovah Jireh, and burn it in hell forever and forever!

Forgive us, good Lord; we know not what we say!

Bewildered we are and passion-tossed, mad with the madness of a mobbed and mocked and murdered people; straining at the armposts of Thy throne, we raise our shackled hands and charge Thee, God, by the bones of our stolen fathers, by the tears of our dead mothers, by the very blood of Thy crucified Christ: What meaneth this? Tell us the plan; give us the sign!

Keep not Thou silent, O God!

Sit not longer blind, Lord God, deaf to our prayer and dumb to our dumb suffering. Surely Thou, too, art not white, O Lord, a pale, bloodless, heartless thing!

Ah! Christ of all the Pities!

Forgive the thought! Forgive these wild, blasphemous words! Thou art still the God of our black fathers and in Thy Soul's Soul sit some soft darkenings of the evening, some shadowings of the velvet night.

But whisper — speak — call, great God, for Thy silence is white terror to our hearts! The way, O God, show us the way and point us the path!

Whither? North is greed and South is blood; within, the coward, and without. the liar. Whither? To death?

Amen! Welcome, dark sleep!

Whither? To life? But not this life, dear God, not this. Let the cup pass from us, tempt us not beyond our strength, for there is that clamoring and that clawing within, to whose voice we would not listen, yet shudder lest we must —

and it is red. Ah! dear God! It is a red and awful shape.
Selah!
In yonder East trembles a star.
Vengeance is Mine; I will repay, saith the Lord!
Thy Will, O Lord, be done!
Kyrie Eleison!
Lord, we have done these pleading, wavering words.
We beseech Thee to hear us, good Lord!
We bow our heads and hearken soft to the sobbing of women and little children.
We beseech Thee to hear us, good Lord!
Our voices sink in silence and in night.
Hear us, good Lord!
In night, O God of a godless land!
Amen!
In silence, O Silent God.
Selah!

Excerpt: DARKWATER (N. Y., Harcourt, Brace & World, Inc., 1920)

THE CRISIS

1910—1934... Dr. Du Bois' profound understanding of the color-line plus his gift of expressing the questions of the day in terms which are easily understood by the average man made him a spokesman for the cause of the Negro in America and for colored peoples in many parts of the world. In 1910, Dr. Du Bois founded *The Crisis* as the official propaganda organ of the National Association for the Advancement of Colored People. Its original circulation of 1,000 grew to 100,000 by 1918. Through the pages of *The Crisis,* Dr. Du Bois expressed himself on every aspect of the race problem, voicing the new aspirations of American Negroes... At the same time, it offended conservative attitudes of many whites and Negroes. The excerpts which appear in this section express the views of Dr. Du Bois on a time which encompassed the First World War; its aftermath; the growth of colonial imperialism, and the birth of the First Socialist State.

THE FIRST YEARS: 1910—1914

The object of this publication is to set forth those facts and arguments which show the danger of race prejudice, particularly as manifested today toward colored people. It takes its name from the fact that the editors believe that this is a critical time in the history of the advancement of men. Catholicity and tolerance, reason and forbearance can today make the world-old dream of human brotherhood approach realization; while bigotry and prejudice, emphasized race consciousness and force can repeat the awful history of the contact of nations and groups in the past. We strive for this higher and broader vision of Peace and Good Will.

Human contact, human acquaintanceship, human sympathy are the great solvents of human problems. Separate school children by wealth and the result is class misunderstanding and hatred. Separate them by race and the result is war. Separate them by color and they grow up without learning the tremendous truth that it is impossible to judge the mind of a man by the color of his face. Back of this demand for the segregation of black folk in public institutions, or the segregation of any class, is almost always a shirking of responsibility on the part of the public — a desire to put off on somebody else the work of social uplift, while they themselves enjoy its results. . . .

The argument, then, for color discrimination in schools and in public institutions is an argument against democracy and an attempt to shift public responsibility. . . .

Some good friends of the cause we represent fear agitation. They say: "Do not agitate — do not make a noise; work." They add: "Agitation is destructive or at best negative — what is wanted is positive constructive work."

Such honest critics mistake the function of agitation. A toothache is agitation. Is a toothache a good thing? No. Is it therefore useless? No. It is supremely useful, for it tells the body of decay and death. Without it the body would suffer unknowingly. It would think: All is well, when lo! danger lurks.

1910 · vol 1

THE WOMAN

In the land of the Heavy Laden came once a dreary day. And the King who sat upon the Great White Throne raised up his eyes and saw afar off how the hills around were hot with hostile feet, and the sound of the mocking of his enemies struck anxiously on the King's ears, for the King loved his enemies. So the King lifted up his hand and in the glittering silence spake softly, saying, "Call the servants of the King."

Then the herald stepped before the armpost of the throne and cried: "Thus saith the High and Mighty One, whose name is Holy: the servants of the King!"

Now, of the servants of the King there were a hundred and forty-four thousand — tried men and brave, brawny of arm and quick in wit; aye, too, and women of wisdom and marvelous in beauty and grace. And yet on this drear day when the King called, their ears were thick with the dust of the enemy, their eyes were blinded with the flashing of his spears, and they hid their faces in dread silence and moved not, even at the King's behest. So the herald called again. And the servants cowered in very shame, but none came forth. But the third blast of the herald struck upon a woman's heart, afar.

And the woman straightway left her baking and sweeping and the rattle of tins. And the woman straightway left her chatting and gossiping and the sewing of garments.

And the woman stood before the King, saying, "The servant of thy servants, O Lord."

Then the King smiled, smiled wondrously, so that the setting sun burst through the clouds and the hearts of the King's men dried hard within them. And the low-voiced King said, so low that even they that listened heard not well: "Go smite me mine enemies that they cease to do evil in my sight."

And the woman quailed and trembled. Three times she lifted up her eyes unto the hills and saw the heathen whirling onward in their rage. And seeing she shrank, three times she shrank and crept to the King's feet.

"O King," she cried, "I am but a woman."

And the King answered: "Go then, mother of men."

And the woman said, "Nay, King, but I am still a maid."

Whereat the King cried: "O Maid made Man, thou shall be Bride of God."

And yet the third time the woman shrank at the thunder in her ears, and whispered: "Dear God, I am black."

And the King spake not, but swept the veiling of his face aside and lifted up the light of his countenance upon her and lo! it was black.

So the woman went forth on the hills of God to do battle for the King on that drear day in the land of the Heavy Laden, when the heathen raged and imagined a vain thing.

1911 · vol 2

THE CORONATION

George V. has been duly crowned King, Emperor and so forth. There was not at the coronation any special attempt, we understand, to emphasize the fact that the British Empire is predominantly colored.

The typical American is an octoroon or, counting the

islands, a mulatto; but the typical Britisher is only one-eighth white. Of the 450,000,000 of beings under the Union Jack only 54,000,000 are white. Next to them come 300,000,000 yellow, brown and black Asiatics, and British Africa with perhaps 100,000,000 Blacks and mixed bloods.

The coming world man is colored. For the handful of whites in this world to dream that they with their present declining birth rate can ever inherit the earth and hold the darker millions in perpetual subjection is the wildest of wild dreams. Humanity is the goal of all good, and no single race, whatever its color or deeds, can disinherit God's anointed peoples.

1911 · vol 11

MODEST ME

The editor of *The Crisis* assumes to be a fairly modest man as modesty goes in these trumpeting times; but with some diffidence he admits to a swelling of pardonable pride at a certain occurrence in South Carolina which the papers of that realm, with somewhat singular unanimity, have omitted to notice.

Some time since — to be exact, in 1901 — the editor and certain other persons (among them the Hon. Woodrow Wilson,* then unknown to a newer kind of fame) were asked to write on "Reconstruction" for the *Atlantic Monthly*. The editor concocted an article which he liked quite well, and in turn the *Atlantic Monthly* was persuaded to publish it. It was called "The Freedman's Bureau." It caused no stir in the world, but the editor kept it carefully in his archives to gloat over now and then in the fastnesses of his study when his family had retired. Very well.

* Woodrow Wilson: 28th President of the United States, 1913—21

Some time in 1911 the Wade Hampton Chapter of the United Daughters of the Confederacy offered a medal to the student of the University of South Carolina writing the best article on 'The Freedman's Bureau." Mr. Colin W. Covington, of Bennettsville, S.C., won the coveted prize, and his essay was published in the *Columbia State,* January 28, 1912.

Imagine, now, the editor's gratification on reading this work of genius to discover that nearly one-half of the essay, and that the important and concluding half, was the editor's own work from his Atlantic essay of 1901! A single quotation will indicate more clearly this new instance of racial concord . . . or two or three pages, but let us forbear. Were the editor a grasping man he might (either for himself or for his race) ask to have a large share of that medal clipped from the proud young Southern breast that bears it and pinned on his own. But no. Sufficient be the secret sense of desert and warmest flattery, and the editor yields to vanity only to the extent of bringing all this to the attention of his assiduous friend, the Charleston *News and Courier,* whose frequent sallies have in the past caused him much innocent amusement.

1912 · vol 3

THE CHILDREN'S NUMBER

Of Children

This is the Children's Number, and as it has grown and developed in the editor's hesitating hands, it has in some way come to seem a typical rather than a special number. Indeed, there is a sense in which all numbers and all words of a magazine of ideas must point to the child — to that vast immortality and wide sweep and infinite possibility which the child represents. As men of old said:

43

"And whosoever shall offend one of these little ones ...
it is better for him that a millstone were hanged about
his neck, and he were cast into the sea."

Of the Giving of Life

And yet the mothers and fathers and the men and women
of our race must often pause and ask: Is it worth while?

Ought children be born to us?

Have we a right to make human souls face what we
face today?

The answer is clear: if the great battle of human right
against poverty, against disease, against color prejudice
is to be won, it must be won not in our day, but in the day
of our children's children. Ours is the blood and dust of
battle, theirs the rewards of victory. If then they are not
there because we have not brought them to the world,
then we have been the guiltiest factor in conquering ourselves. It is our duty then to accomplish the immortality
of black blood in order that the day may come in this dark
world when poverty shall be abolished, privilege based
on individual desert, and the color of a man's skin be no
bar to the outlook of his soul.

Of the Shielding Arm

If then it is our duty as honest colored men and women
battling for a great principle to bring not aimless rafts of
children to the world, but as many as, with reasonable
sacrifice, we can train to largest manhood, what in its
inner essence shall that training be, particularly in its
beginning?

Our first impulse is to shield our children absolutely.
Look at these happy, innocent faces: for most of them
there is as yet no shadow, no thought of a color-line. The
world is beautiful and good, and life is joy. But we know

only too well that beyond the disillusionment and hardening that lurk for every human soul there is that extra hurting which, even when unconscious, with fiendish refinement of cruelty waits on each corner to shadow the joy of our children; if they are backward or timid, there is the sneer; if they are forward, there is repression; the problems of playmates and amusements are infinite, and street and school and church have that extra hazard of pain and temptation that spells hell to our babies.

The first temptation then is to shield the child; to hedge it about that it may not know and will not dream. Then, when we can no longer wholly shield, to indulge and pamper and coddle, as though in this dumb way to compensate. From this attitude comes the multitude of our spoiled, wayward, disappointed children; and must we not blame ourselves? For while the motive was pure and the outer menace undoubted, is shielding and indulgence the way?

Of the Grim Thrust

Some parents realizing this, leave their children to sink or swim in this sea of race prejudice. They thrust them forth grimly into school or street, and let them learn as they may from brutal fact. Out of this may come strength, poise, self-dependence, and out of it, too, may come bewilderment, cringing deception and self-distrust. It is, all said, a brutal, unfair method, and in its way as bad as shielding and indulgence. Why not rather face the facts and tell the truth? Your child is wiser than you think.

The Frank Truth

The truth lies between extremes. It is wrong to introduce the child to race consciousness prematurely. It is dangerous to let that consciousness grow without intelligent guidance. With every step of dawning intelligence explanation — frank, free guiding explanation — must come. The day will arrive when mother must explain gently but clearly why the little girls next door do not want to play with "niggers"; what the real cause is of the teachers' unsympathetic attitude, and how people may ride on the backs of street cars and the smoker end of trains, and still be people, honest high-minded souls.

Remember, too, that in such frank explanation you are speaking in nine cases out of ten to a good deal clearer understanding than you think, and that the child mind has what your tired soul may have lost faith in — the power and the glory.

The Power and the Glory

Out of little unspoiled souls rise up wonderful resources and healing balm. Once the colored child understands the world's attitude and the shameful wrong of it, you have furnished it with a great life motive — a power and impulse toward good, which is the mightiest thing man has. How many white folks would give their own souls if they might graft into their children's souls a great, moving, guiding ideal!

With this power there comes in the transfiguring soul of childhood the glory: the vision of accomplishment — the lofty ideal. Once let the strength of the motive work, and it becomes the life task of the parent to guide and shape the ideal; to raise it from resentment and revenge, to dignity and self-respect, to breadth and accomplishment, to human service; to beat back every thought of cringing and surrender.

Here, at last, we can speak with no hesitating, with no lack of faith. For we know that as the world grows better there will be realized in our children's lives that for which we fight unfalteringly but vainly now.

1912 · vol 4

In popular imagination the drawing of the color-line is a solemn performance done after grave deliberation by perfectly unselfish men, for lofty purpose and for vast contemplative ends.

In the face of such conception what shall be said at the trickery, lying and chicanery that has marked the drawing of racial lines in the American Bar Association? Why should there be such hiding and deception? Is somebody ashamed of something? Is it a discreditable and disreputable thing to say to a man: "If you are black you cannot join the American Bar Association?" If it is not a nasty and unworthy discrimination to say this, why not say it flatly and first, instead of:

1. Hushing the matter up.
2. Asking the colored man "quietly" to resign.
3. Seeking to break law and precedent in declaring a member not a member, but a "candidate" for membership.
4 Endless and disingenuous explanations, avowing the broadest charity and highest motives.
5. The sending out of new membership blanks calling for information as to the "race and sex" of candidates before the association had authorized such action.
6. The admission that such blanks were sent without authority, but that the matter would be duly reported when it never was reported.
7. A secret bargain which one of the most prominent lawyers in the United States thus describes:

The resolution was presented by ex-President and ex-Secretary of War Dickinson, seconded by an Illinois man... and then the previous question was instantly moved — all evidently in pursuance of a prearranged plan. I need say no more than that after about fifteen minutes of absolute riot the chairman ... declared the resolution adopted and declared the meeting adjourned. What was actually said or done in the interval it is impossible to tell. A dozen or twenty men were on their feet constantly yelling for recognition by the chair, and the exclusionist gang was yelling "question!" "question!" all over the hall, and it was simply a mob. So far as I could judge, when the question was finally put on the resolution, after I had got recognized for a point of order which the chair conceded but gave us no benefit of, there were about 50 "noes" in a meeting of about 500.

In the name of civilization, what were 450 men so ashamed of that they could not step into the light of day and do frankly and openly that which took three official lies, two infractions of the common law, a corrupt bargain and a "mob" to allow the associated bar of the nation to accomplish?

Does anyone suspect that here, as elsewhere, in this land of the free, a number of eminent gentlemen wished opportunity to do a dirty trick in the dark so as to stand in the light and yell: "We give the black man every chance and yet look at him!"

1912 · vol 4

THE LAST WORD IN POLITICS

Before another number of *The Crisis* appears the next President of the United States will have been elected. We have, therefore, this last word to colored voters and their friends.

Those who have scanned our advertising pages this month and last have noted an unusual phenomenon: the three great political parties have in this way been appealing to the colored vote for support. They have done this out of no love to this magazine, but because they needed the publicity which this magazine alone could give and because they knew that our news columns and editorial pages were not for sale. We commend these advertisements to our readers' notice. They are the last word of political appeal and they are undoubtedly sincere.

Taking them now and comparing and weighing them, what is the net result? The Republican Party emphasizes its past relations with the Negro, the recent appointments to office, and warns against the disfranchisement and caste system of the Democratic South. The weak point in this argument is that without the consent of Republican Presidents, Republican Congresses and a Republican Supreme Court, Southern disfranchisement could not survive a single day.

The Progressive Party stresses its platform of social reform, so admirable in many respects, and points to the recognition given in its party councils to the Northern Negro voter. The weak point here is the silence over the fact that Theodore Roosevelt,* the perpetrator of the Brownsville outrage, has added to that blunder the Chicago disfranchisement and is appealing to the South for white votes on this platform.

The Democratic Party appeals for colored votes on the ground that other parties have done and are doing precisely the things that the Democratic Party is accused of doing against the Negro, and this in spite of the fact that these parties receive the bulk of the Negro vote. If, therefore, the Negro expects Democratic help and support, why does he not give the Democrats his vote? The weak point here is that the invitation is at best negative; the Negro is asked to take a leap in the dark without specific promises as to what protection he may expect after the Democrats are in power.

* Theodore Roosevelt: 26th President of the United States, 1901—09

In none of these cases, therefore, is the invitation satisfactory. Nevertheless, because the Socialists, with their manly stand for human rights irrespective of color, are at present out of the calculation, the Negro voter must choose between these three parties. He is asked virtually to vote

1. For a party which has promised and failed.
2. For a party which has failed and promised.
3. For a party which merely promises.

We sympathize with those faithful old black voters who will always vote the Republican ticket. We respect their fidelity but not their brains. We can understand those who, despite the unspeakable Theodore Roosevelt, accept his platform which is broad on all subjects except the greatest — human rights. This we can understand, but we cannot follow.

We sincerely believe that even in the face of promises disconcertingly vague, and in the face of the solid caste-ridden South, it is better to elect Woodrow Wilson President of the United States and prove once for all if the Democratic Party dares to be Democratic when it comes to black men. It was proven that it can be in many Northern States and cities. Can it be in the nation? We hope so and we are willing to risk a trial.

1912 · vol 4

THE TRUTH

What this nation and this world needs is a Renaissance of reverence for the truth. If *The Crisis* stands for one thing above others, it is emphasis of this fact, and it is here that we have to differ with some of our best friends. We are here to tell the essential facts about the condition of the Negro in the United States. Not all the facts, of course — one can never tell everything about anything. Human communication must always involve some selection and emphasis. Nevertheless, in such selection and emphasis there can be two attitudes as different as the poles. One attitude assumes that the truth ought to be as one person or race wants it and then proceeds to make the facts prove this thesis. The other attitude strives without undue assumption of any kind to show the true implication of the existing facts. The first attitude is that of nearly all the organs of public opinion in the United States on the Negro problem. They have assumed, and for the most part firmly believe, that the Negro is an undesirable race destined to eventual extinction of some kind. Every essential fact and situation is therefore colored and grouped to support this thesis, and when stubborn facts appear that simply will not support this thesis there is almost complete silence.

Few Americans, many Negroes, do not realize how widespread and dangerous this disregard of truth in relation to the Negro has become and how terrible is its influence. Sir Harry Johnston, a great Englishman, was recently invited to furnish his views on the Negro to a popular American magazine. When these articles were written and seemed favorable to the black man the magazine paid for them and suppressed them. Jane Addams* was asked to write on the Progressive Party for *McClure's Magazine.* Her defense of Negro rights was, with her consent, left out, and appeared in *The Crisis* last month. Charles Edward Stowe offered his "Religion of Slavery" to the *Outlook.* It was returned not as untrue but "unwise."

Many persons who know these things defend this attitude toward the truth. They say when matters are bad do not emphasize their badness, but seek the encouraging aspects. If the situation of the Negro is difficult strive to better it, but do not continually harp on the difficulties. The trouble with this attitude is that it assumes that every-

* Jane Addams: U.S. educator, social worker and writer

body knows the truth; that everybody knows the terrible plight of the black man in America. But how do they know it when the organs of public information are dumb? Would anybody ever suspect by reading the *Outlook* that educated property-holding Negroes are disfranchised? Would any future generation dream by reading the *Southern Workman* that 5,000 Negroes had been murdered without trial during its existence? What right have we to assume intuitive and perfect knowledge of truth in this one problem, while in myriads of other human problems we bend every energy and strain every nerve to make the truth known to all? Is there not room in the nation for one organ devoted to a fair interpretation of the essential facts concerning the Negro? There certainly is, even if the silence and omissions of the public press were quite unconscious; but how much more is the need when the misrepresentation is deliberate? In the recent Congress of Hygiene in Washington there was sent from Philadelphia a chart alleging in detail the grossest and most unspeakable immorality against the whole Negro race. Colored folk led by F. H. M. Murray protested. The secretary immediately had the offensive lie withdrawn and said: "I am sorry the chart ever found a place there, but I should be more sorry if the colored people had not protested." Here is the honest man's attitude: "I am sorry colored Americans are treated unjustly, but I should be more sorry if they did not let the truth be known."

Granted that the duty of chronicling ten mob murders a month, a dozen despicable insults and outrages, is not pleasant occupation, is the unpleasantness the fault of *The Crisis* or of the nation that perpetrates such dastardly outrages? "Why," said one of our critics, "if I should tell my white guests of the difficulties, rebuffs and discouragements of colored folk right here in Boston, they would go away and never visit us again. If, however, I tell how nicely the Negroes are getting on, they give money." Yes! And if your object is money you do right, but if your object is truth, then you should not only tell your visitors the truth but pursue them with it as they run.

True it is that this high duty cannot always be followed. True it is that often we must sit dumb before the golden calf, but is not this the greater call for a voice to cry in the wilderness, for reiterated declaration that the way of the Lord is straight and not a winding, crooked, cunning thing?

1912 · vol 5

THE JIM CROW ARGUMENT

The chairman of the committee in the Missouri legislature which is engineering the Jim Crow car bill has evolved this unanswerable syllogism:

1. Negroes should not object to being separated on the trains by "just a small railing."
2. If they do object it shows that they are averse to associating with themselves.
3. If they insist on associating with whites, it shows that they want "social equality!"

The argument of our learned and astute solon not only proves his case, but it proves so much in addition as to destroy his argument.

If poor people object to being separated from rich people, does it prove a wild desire for the society of say, Mrs. Ponsonby de Thompkyns or simply righteous indignation at having manhood measured by wealth?

If Jews object to the Ghetto and the pale, does it prove them ashamed of themselves or afraid of those oppressors who find oppression easier when the victims are segregated and helpless?

The modern fight for human freedom is the fight of the individual man to be judged on his own merits and not to be saddled with the sins of a class for which he is not

53

responsible. The favorite device of the devil, ancient and modern, is to force a human being into a more or less artificial class, accuse the class of unnamed and unnamable sin, and then damn any individual in the alleged class, however innocent he may be.

This is the medieval tyranny which the South has revived in Jim Crow legislation and which Missouri is striving for. The South fulminates against dirt, crime and bad manners and then herds in the Jim Crow car the clean and unclean and the innocent and guilty and the decent and indecent. Separation is impossible in a democracy. It means segregation, subordination and tyranny.

Social equality? Of course we want social equality. Social equality is the right to demand the treatment of men from your fellow man. To ask less is to acknowledge your own lack of manhood.

1913 · vol 5

INTERMARRIAGE

Few groups of people are forced by their situation into such cruel dilemmas as American Negroes. Nevertheless they must not allow anger or personal resentment to dim their clear vision.

Take, for instance, the question of the intermarrying of white and black folk; it is a question that colored people seldom discuss. It is about the last of the social problems over which they are disturbed, because they so seldom face it in fact or in theory. Their problems are problems of work and wages, of the right to vote, of the right to travel decently, of the right to frequent places of public amusement, of the right to public security.

White people, on the other hand, for the most part profess to see but one problem: "Do you want your sister to marry a nigger?" Sometimes we are led to wonder if they are lying about their solicitude on this point; and if they are not, we are led to ask why under present laws anybody should be compelled to marry any person whom she does not wish to marry?

This brings us to the crucial question: so far as the present advisability of intermarrying between white and colored people in the United States is concerned, both races are practically in complete agreement. Colored folk marry colored folk and white marry white, and the exceptions are very few.

Why not then stop the exceptions? For three reasons: physical, social and moral.

1. For the *physical* reason that to prohibit such intermarriage would be publicly to acknowledge that black blood is a physical taint — a thing that no decent, self-respecting black man can be asked to admit.

2. For the *social* reason that if two full-grown responsible human beings of any race and color propose to live together as man and wife, it is only social decency not simply to allow, but to compel them to marry. Let those people who have yelled themselves purple in the face over Jack Johnson* just sit down and ask themselves this question: Granted that Johnson and Miss Cameron proposed to live together, was it better for them to be legally married or not? We know what the answer of the Bourbon South is. We know that they would rather uproot the foundations of decent society than to call the consorts of their brothers, sons and fathers their legal wives. We infinitely prefer the methods of Jack Johnson to those of the brother of Governor Mann of Virginia.

3. The *moral* reason for opposing laws against intermarriage is the greatest of all: such laws leave the colored girl absolutely helpless before the lust of white men. It reduces colored women in the eyes of the law to the

* Jack Johnson: Negro prize fighter and world heavy-weight champion

status of dogs. Low as the white girl falls, she can compel her seducer to marry her. If it were proposed to take this last defense from poor white working girls, can you not hear the screams of the "white slave" defenders? What have these people to say to laws that propose to create in the United States 5,000,000 women, the ownership of whose bodies no white man is bound to respect?

Note these arguments, my brothers and sisters, and watch your State legislatures. This winter will see a determined attempt to insult and degrade us by such non-intermarriage laws. We must kill them, not because we are anxious to marry white men's sisters, but because we are determined that white men shall let our sisters alone.

1913 · vol 5

HAIL COLUMBIA!

Hail Columbia, Happy Land! Again the glorious traditions of Anglo-Saxon manhood have been upheld! Again the chivalry of American white men has been magnificently vindicated. Down on your knees, black men, and hear the tale with awestruck faces. Learn from the Superior Race. We do not trust our own faltering pen and purblind sight to describe the reception of the suffragists at the capital of the land. We quote from the Southern reporters of the Northern press:

Five thousand women, marching in the woman-suffrage pageant yesterday, practically fought their way foot by foot up Pennsylvania Avenue, through a surging mass of humanity that completely defied the Washington police, swamped the marchers, and broke their procession into little companies. The women, trudging stoutly along under great difficulties, were able to complete their march only when troops of cavalry from Fort Myer were rushed into

Washington to take charge of Pennsylvania Avenue. No inauguration has ever produced such scenes, which in many instances amounted to little less than riots.

More than 100 persons, young and old, of both sexes, were crushed and trampled in the uncontrollable crowd in Pennsylvania Avenue yesterday, while two ambulances of the Emergency Hospital came and went constantly for six hours, always impeded and at times actually opposed, so that doctor and driver literally had to fight their way to give succor to the injured.

Hoodlums, many of them in uniform, leaned forward till their cigarettes almost touched the women's faces while blowing smoke in their eyes, and the police said not a word, not even when every kind of insult was hurled.

To the white-haired women the men shouted continuously: "Granny! granny! We came to see chickens, not hens! Go home and sit in the corner!" To the younger women they yelled: "Say, what you going to do tonight? Can't we make a date?" and the police only smiled. The rowdies jumped on the running boards of the automobiles and snatched the flags from the elderly women, and they attempted to pull the girls from the floats.

Wasn't it glorious? Does it not make you burn with shame to be a mere black man when such mighty deeds are done by the Leaders of Civilization? Does it not make you "ashamed of your race?" Does is not make you "want to be white?"

And do you know (we are almost ashamed to say it) the Negro again lost a brilliant opportunity to rise in his "imitative" way. Ida Husted Harper says:

We made the closest observation along the entire line and not in one instance did we hear a colored man make a remark, although there were thousands of them.

Another white woman writes:

I wish to speak a word in favor of the colored people during the suffrage parade. Not one of them was boisterous or rude as with great difficulty we passed along the unprotected avenue. The difference between them and those insolent, bold white men was remarkable. They were quiet and respectable and earnest, and seemed sorry for the indignities which were incessantly heaped upon us. There were few policemen to protect us as we made our first parade in Washington, and the dignified silence of the colored people and the sympathy in their faces was a great contrast to those who should have known better. I thank them in the name of all the women for their kindness.

Now look at that! Good Lord! has the Negro *no* sense? Can he grasp no opportunity?

But let him not think to gain by any such tactics. The South sees his game and is busy promoting bills to prevent his marrying any wild-eyed suffragette who may be attracted by his pusillanimous decency. Already the Ohio legislature has been flooded by forged petitions from a "Negro advancement society of New York" to push the intermarriage bill!

No, sir! White men are on the firing line, and if they don't want white women for wives they will at least keep them for prostitutes. Beat them back, keep them down; flatter them, call them "visions of loveliness" and tell them that the place for woman is in the home, even if she hasn't got a home. If she is homely or poor or made the mistake of being born with brains, and begins to protest at the doll's house or the bawdy house, kick her and beat her and insult her until in terror she slinks back to her kennel or walks the midnight streets. Don't give in; don't give her power; don't give her a vote whatever you do. Keep the price of women down; make them weak and cheap.

Shall the time ever dawn in this Land of the Brave

when a free white American citizen may not buy as many women as his purse permits? Perish the thought and Hail Columbia, Happy Land!

1913 · vol 5

PEACE

At the coming meeting of the peace societies at St. Louis the question of peace between civilized and backward peoples will not probably be considered. The secretary of the New York Peace Society writes us that "Our peace congresses have not dealt in the past with the relations of civilized and non-civilized people"; and he thinks that largely on this account "our American congresses have been more dignified and more influential than those held abroad."

We are not sure about that word "influential," but there is no doubt about the dignity of the American peace movement. It has been so dignified and aristocratic that it has been often most difficult for the humbler sort of folk to recognize it as the opponent of organized murder.

At a recent meeting of the New York Peace Society the war in the Balkans was eulogized and applauded, and the president stated that "when we advocate peace" it is for nations "worthy of it!"

Such a peace movement belies its name. Peace today, if it means anything, means the stopping of the slaughter of the weaker by the stronger in the name of Christianity and culture. The modern lust for land and slaves in Africa, Asia and the South Seas is the greatest and almost the only cause of war between the so-called civilized peoples. For such "colonial" aggression and "imperial" expansion England, France, Germany, Russia and Austria are straining every nerve to arm themselves; against such policies Japan and China are arming desperately. And yet the American peace movement thinks it bad policy to take up this problem of machine guns, natives and rubber, and wants "constructive" work in "arbitration treaties and international law."

For our part we think that a little less dignity and dollars and a little more humanity would make the peace movement in America a great democratic philanthropy instead of an aristocratic refuge.

AN OPEN LETTER TO WOODROW WILSON

Sir: On the occasion of your inauguration as President of the United States, *The Crisis* took the liberty of addressing to you an open letter. *The Crisis* spoke for no inconsiderable part of ten millions of human beings, American born, American citizens. . . .

Sir, you have now been President of the United States for six months and what is the result? It is no exaggeration to say that every enemy of the Negro race is greatly encouraged; that every man who dreams of making the Negro race a group of menials and pariahs is alert and hopeful. They are evidently assuming that their theory of the place and destiny of the Negro race is the theory of your administration. They and others are assuming this because not a single act and not a single word of yours since election has given anyone reason to infer that you have the slightest interest in the colored people or desire to alleviate their intolerable position. A dozen worthy Negro officials have been removed from office, and you have nominated but one black man for office, and he, such a contemptible cur, that his very nomination was an insult to every Negro in the land.

To this negative appearance of indifference has been added positive action on the part of your advisers, with or without your knowledge, which constitutes the gravest attack on the liberties of our people since emancipation. Public segregation of civil servants in government employ, necessarily involving personal insult and humiliation, has for the first time in history been made the policy of the United States government.

In the Treasury and Post Office Departments colored clerks have been herded to themselves as though they were not human beings. We are told that one colored clerk who could not actually be segregated on account of the nature of his work has consequently had a cage built around him to separate him from his white companions of many years. Mr. Wilson, do you know these things? Are you responsible for them? Did you advise them? Do you not know that no other group of American citizens has ever been treated in this way and that no President of the United States ever dared to propose such treatment? Here is a plain, flat, disgraceful spitting in the face of people whose darkened countenances are already dark with the slime of insult. Do you consent to this, President Wilson? Do you believe in it? Have you been able to persuade yourself that national insult is best for a people struggling into self-respect?

President Wilson, we do not, we cannot believe this. *The Crisis* still clings to the conviction that a vote for Woodrow Wilson was NOT a vote for segregation. But whether it was or not segregation is going to be resented as it ought to be resented by the colored people. We would not be men if we did not resent it. The policy adopted, whether with your consent or knowledge or not, is an indefensible attack on a people who have in the past been shamefully humiliated. There are foolish people who think that such policy has no limit and that lynching, Jim Crowism, segregation and insult are to be permanent institutions in America.

We have appealed in the past, Mr. Wilson, to you as a man and statesman; to your sense of fairness and broad cosmopolitan outlook on the world. We renew this appeal and to it we venture to add some plain considerations of political expediency.

We black men still vote. In spite of the fact that the triumph of your party last fall was possible only because Southern white men have, through our disfranchisement, from twice to seven times the political power of Northern white men — notwithstanding this, we black men of the North have a growing nest egg of 500,000 ballots, and ballots that are counted, which no sane party can ignore. Does your Mr. Burleson expect the Democratic Party to carry New York, New Jersey, Pennsylvania, Ohio, Indiana, Illinois, by 200,000 votes? If he does will it not be well for him to remember that there are 237,942 black voters in these States. We have been trying to tell these voters that the Democratic Party wants their votes. Have we been wrong, Mr. Wilson? Have we assumed too great and quick a growth of intelligence in the party that once made slavery its cornerstone?

In view of all this, we beg to ask the President of the United States and the leader of the Democratic Party a few plain questions:

1. Do you want Negro votes?
2. Do you think that a Jim Crow civil service will get these votes?
3. Is your Negro policy to be dictated by Tillman and Vardaman?
4. Are you going to appoint black men to office on the same terms that you choose white men?

This is information, Mr. Wilson, which we are very anxious to have.

The Crisis advocated sincerely and strongly your election to the Presidency. *The Crisis* has no desire to be compelled to apologize to its constituency for this course. But at the present rate it looks as though some apology or explanation was going to be in order very soon.

We are still hoping that present indications are deceptive. We are still trying to believe that the President of the United States is the President of 10,000,000, as well as of 90,000,000, and that though the 10,000,000 are black and poor, he is too honest and cultured a gentleman to yield to the clamors of ignorance and prejudice and hatred. We are still hoping all this, Mr. Wilson, but hope deferred maketh the heart sick.

1913 · vol 6

THE FRUIT OF THE TREE

Let no one for a moment mistake that the present increased attack on the Negro along all lines is but the legitimate fruit of that long campaign for subserviency and surrender which a large party of Negroes have fathered now some twenty years. It is not necessary to question the motives of these men nor to deny that their insistence on thrift and saving has had its large and beneficent effect. But, on the other hand, only the blind and foolish can fail to see that a continued campaign in every nook and corner of this land, preaching to people white and colored, that the Negro is chiefly to blame for his condition, that he must not insist on his rights, that he should not take part in politics, that Jim Crowism is defensible and even advantageous, that he should humbly bow to the storm until the lordly white man grants him clemency — the fruit of this disgraceful doctrine is disfranchisement, segregation, lynching. . . .

Fellow Negroes, is it not time to be men? Is it not time to strike back when we are struck? Is it not high time to hold up our heads and clench our teeth and swear by the Eternal God we will NOT be slaves, and that no aider, abetter and teacher of slavery in any shape or guise can longer lead us?

1913 · vol 6

We will suppose, dear reader, that you are free, white and twenty-one; that you are reasonably patriotic and would rather the world grew better than worse.

What should be your first duty? Will you pardon us for suggesting membership in the National Association for the Advancement of Colored People as your first and greatest duty?

Does the advice sound a bit grotesque and myopic?

Pause, then, and consider:

Freedom is a state of mind: a spiritual unchoking of the wells of human power and superhuman love. Is there anything in America that is so strangling brotherhood and narrowing humanity and encouraging hatred, lust and murder as race prejudice? Is there any conceivable crime that it does not daily excuse? Any conceivable inhumanity that it may not deify? If you want freedom, then join this association and fight race hatred.

You are "white." You want to remain "white." You want your children to be "white." Very well. Your wish on this point may seem to some of us of slightly less than infinite importance and yet this is your wish, and the wish of any human being must be respected.

But do you realize that the one certain way to insure a future mulatto world is to despise black folk? Do you realize that if you make this world a hell for Africans and Chinese and Malays that the result will be the rapid disappearance of race differentiation and that, too, largely and predominantly by amalgamation?

If then you want to preserve the special characteristics of white peoples, make it possible for darker peoples to preserve their racial characteristics without loss of freedom and self-respect.

You are twenty-one — i. e., you can vote. Or at least you think you can. Or if you are really wise you know what a farce voting is in this land. Why? Because a

Southern voter has from twice to seven times the power of a Northern voter and South Carolina far outweighs Illinois in political significance. Because political democracy cannot be linked with industrial despotism, else the result is the rule of the rich. Now industrial despotism is founded on slavery and peonage, rack rent and low wages. Negroes were slaves, they are peons, they are rack rented and receive less than can support them in decency. Against them white workingmen must compete and the votes stolen from Negroes are used by white capitalists to keep the laborer in bondage. Is your vote safe then as long as disfranchisement and peonage are in the land?

Wherefore, as one who is "free, white and twenty-one," come and join us and help accomplish freedom, safeguard legitimate pride of being and make democracy real.

1914 · vol 7

THE PHILOSOPHY OF MR. DOLE

We publish very gladly Mr. Dole's criticism of *The Crisis*, because of our deep respect for the writer and because he voices a real and vital disagreement with our policy.... This, briefly, is his thesis: "Don't antagonize, don't be bitter; say the conciliatory thing; make friends and do not repel them; insist on and emphasize the cheerful and good and dwell as little as possible on wrong and evil."

The Crisis does not believe in this policy so far as the present status of the American Negro problem is concerned. We could imagine many social problems, and many phases in a particular problem, when the watchful waiting, the tactfully conciliatory attitude would be commendable and worth while. At other times it would be suicidal and this, in our opinion, is one of the times.

It was ever so. When the Hebrew prophets cried aloud there were respectable persons by the score who said:

"Unfortunate exaggeration!"

"Unnecessary feeling!"

"Ungodly bitterness!"

Yet the jeremiads were needed to redeem a people. When the abolitionists began, not simply to say, but to act as if slavery were a "covenant with hell," there were plenty of timid souls "on the fence, hesitating," who scrambled down hastily on the popular side and were willing to lynch Garrison and ostracize Phillips.

All this might be beside the mark if we had not already tried Mr. Dole's prescriptions. For now nearly twenty years we have made of ourselves mudsills for the feet of this Western world. We have echoed and applauded every shameful accusation made against 10,000,000 victims of slavery. Did they call us inferior half-beasts? We nodded our simple heads and whispered: "We is." Did they call our women prostitutes and our children bastards? We smiled and cast a stone at the bruised breasts of our wives and daughters. Did they accuse of laziness 4,000,000 sweating, struggling laborers, half paid and cheated out of much of that? We shrieked: "Ain't it so?" We laughed with them at our color, we joked at our sad past, and we told chicken stories to get alms.

And what was the result? We got "friends." I do not believe any people ever had so many "friends" as the American Negro today! He has nothing but "friends" and may the good God deliver him from most of them, for they are like to lynch his soul.

What is it to be a friend of the Negro? It is to believe in anything for him except, perhaps, total and immediate annihilation. Short of that, good and kind friends of colored folk believe that he is, in Mr. Dooley's charming phrase, "aisily lynched," and ought to be occasionally. Even if 2,662 accused black people have been publicly lynched, burned and mutilated in twenty-eight years (not to mention the murder of perhaps 10,000 other black folk), our friends think we ought not to disturb the good President of these United States because *the wonder is that there is so little killing!*

It is the old battle of the better and the best. The worst foes of Negro manhood today are those compromising friends who are willingly satisfied with even less than half a loaf. They want the Negro educated; but the South objects to Negro colleges. Oh, very well, then, high schools; but the South objects to "literary" training for "niggers!" Dear, dear! Then "industrial" training; but the South objects to training any considerable number of Negroes for industry; it wants them for menial service. Very well, train them as servants and field hands — anything as long as it is "education!" Then we and *The Crisis* rise and say: *"But —"* Our friends raise deprecating hands; they adjust the sofa pillows, shade the light, and say: "Now, now! *Give them the benefit of the doubt!"*

Or we clamor for the right to vote. "Of course you should vote," say our friends. "But," says the South, "they are too ignorant and inexperienced; we will vote for them." "Excellent," cry our friends, "vote for them and guard them in their civil rights." "What's this?" asks the South. "We mean their economic rights," say our friends glibly, "their right to work and get property." "Yes," answers the South calmly, "the right to work, and we'll work them." "But —" cries *The Crisis* and the black man who has been worked long enough. "Sh!" answer our friends. *"You'll halt the procession!"*

That's precisely what we intend to do. For twenty-five years we have let the procession go by until the systematic denial of manhood rights to black men in America is the crying disgrace of the century. We have wrongs, deep and bitter wrongs. There are local and individual exceptions; there are some mitigating circumstances; there is much to be excused; there is much to be said; and yet for the great mass of 10,000,000 Americans of Negro descent these things are true:

We are denied education.

We are driven out of the Church of Christ.

We are forced out of hotels, theatres and public places.

We are publicly labeled like dogs when we travel.

We can seldom get decent employment.

We are forced down to the lowest wage scale.

We pay the highest rent for the poorest homes.

We cannot buy property in decent neighborhoods.

We are held up to ridicule in the press and on the platform and stage.

We are disfranchised.

We are taxed without representation.

We are denied the right to choose our friends or to be chosen by them, but must publicly announce ourselves as social pariahs or be suggestively kicked by the *Survey*.

In law and custom our women have no rights which a white man is bound to respect.

We cannot get justice in the courts.

We are lynched with impunity.

We are publicly, continuously and shamefully insulted from the day of our birth to the day of our death.

And yet we are told not to be "selfconscious"; to lie about the truth in order to make it "come true"; to grapple with the "philosophy of evolution"; and not to make people "feel ugly" by telling them "ugly facts."

Few admire Mr. Dole, personally, more than the editor of *The Crisis*. Mr. Dole is the type of what the American of the future may be: fine in feeling, delicate in touch, sensitive to the subtle beauties of the world. But Mr. Dole's feet never walked the way we tread. He does not know — he cannot conceive this darker world of insult, repression, hunger and murder.

He and Charles William Eliot* and Woodrow Wilson and millions of others have given no encouragement to lynching, except by silence!

* Charles William Eliot: President of Harvard University, 1869—1909

EXCEPT BY SILENCE!

Who ever tried harder than the Negro and his "friends" to use the lie for social betterment? We have lied about the South so strenuously that this may account for the persistent blackness of our faces. Oh, yes: the South is the true, tried friend of Negroes; the South wants them educated; the South detests lynching; the South loves black mammies and buries them handsomely; the little playful antics of mobs are but ebullitions of Anglo-Saxon energy or at worst the faults of "poor white trash," who do not count. Moreover, those who dispute these statements are either meddling white Northerners or impudent Negroes who want to marry white women.

All of this we black folk and our "friends" have been saying glibly and frequently. We were lying, and we knew we were lying, *to make the "falsehood come true"*; but did the world know this? Did we not lull this nation to false security and fatuous insensibility? And is the uneasiness of our friends at the plain talk of *The Crisis* the cause of ugly feeling or the necessary result of ridiculous lies? How far may we indeed meddle with the truth? Where is the boundary line between getting people "to come and believe" what is untrue and telling them on your honor that black is white? We have a sincere desire to see a little brochure by Mr. Dole — with handmade paper, deckle edged and privately printed — on "The Uses of the Lie as a Means of Social Salvation." We would like to distribute a few copies in Heaven among Mr. Dole's Puritan ancestors and listen to the ensuing profanity.

It is the palpable evasions of our friends, and our earnest friends like Mr. Dole, that are most discouraging. When we protest at the plain insult of "negro," Mr. Dole answers that we do not capitalize "white." But white is not the correlative of Negro, as Mr. Dole knows right well. "Black" and "colored" are the correlatives to "white," while Negro is used exactly as the words Malay or German or Jew or Indian are used. To refuse a word so used capitalization is a petty and usually a deliberate insult.

Humanity is progressing toward an ideal; but not, please God, solely by help of men who sit in cloistered ease, hesitate from action and seek sweetness and light; rather we progress today, as in the past, by the soul-torn strength of those who can never sit still and silent while the disinherited and the damned clog our gutters and gasp their lives out on our front porches.

These are the men who go down in the blood and dust of battle. They say ugly things to an ugly world. They spew the lukewarm fence straddlers out of their mouths, like God of old; they cry aloud and spare not; they shout from the housetops, and they make this world so damned uncomfortable with its nasty burden of evil that it tries to get good and does get better.

Evolution is evolving the millennium, but one of the unescapable factors in evolution are the men who hate wickedness and oppression with perfect hatred, who will not equivocate, will not excuse, and will be heard. With the sainted spirits of such as these *The Crisis* would weakly but earnestly stand and cry in the world's four corners of the way; and it claims no man as friend who dare not stand and cry with it.

1914 · vol 8

THE PRIZE FIGHTER

Boxing is an ancient sport. It is mentioned in Homer's *Iliad* and Virgil's *Aeneid* and was a recognized branch of the celebrated Olympic games. During the Middle Ages boxing went out of style among most nations, the preference being given to various encounters with weapons. In England it was revived in the seventeenth century, and fighting with bare fists became a national sport in the eighteenth century. Boxing gloves were invented late in that century, and in the beginning of the nineteenth century, John Jackson (note the prophecy!) became champion and teacher of Lord Byron and other great and titled personages.

Gradually the more brutal features of the sport were eliminated and the eighth Marquess of Queensberry drew up a set of rules in the sixties which have since prevailed.

There is still today some brutality connected with boxing, but as compared with football and boat racing it may be seriously questioned whether boxing deserves to be put in a separate class by reason of its cruelty. Certainly it is a highly civilized pastime as compared with the international game of war which produces so many "heroes" and national monuments.

Despite all this, boxing has fallen into disfavor — into very great disfavor. To see publications like the *New York Times* roll their eyes in shivery horror at the news from Paris (to which it is compelled to give a front page) makes one realize the depths to which we have fallen.

The cause is clear: Jack Johnson, successor of the eighteenth century John Jackson, has outsparred an Irishman. He did it with little brutality, utmost fairness and great good nature. He did not "knock" his opponent senseless. Apparently he did not even try. Neither he nor his race invented prize fighting or particularly like it.

Why then this thrill of national disgust? Because Johnson is black. Of course, some pretend to object to Mr. Johnson's character. But we have yet to hear, in the case of white America, that marital troubles have disqualified prize fighters or ball players or even statesmen. It comes down, then, after all to this unforgivable blackness. Wherefore we conclude that at present prize fighting is very, very immoral, and that we must rely on football and war for pastime until Mr. Johnson retires or permits himself to be "knocked out."

1914 · vol 8

Once upon a time there lay a land in the southern seas; a dark, grim land, walled well against the world. And in that land rose three rivers and a fourth, all flowing out to seek the sea. One river was born amid the Lakes and Mountains of the Moon, sun-kissed, snow-capped, and fled to the northward silent, swiftly; it clambered over the hills and swam the marshes. It threaded the sands — the narrow, choking sands that grew hotter and narrower as it went; yet the river swept on to wider, greener fields, to a laughing plain until through many mouths it burst like a rocket to the Middle Sea with all its myriads of men.

In the wake of the river came dark men creeping, dancing, marching, building, until their pyramids and temples dotted the land and dared the Heavens, and the Thought of their souls and cities was the Beginning of the World.

Far, far away to westward another river leapt and sang and lightly turned its back upon the Sea, rushing to northward. But the grim desert shrieked in its fastnesses crying "Not here!" So the river whirled southward till the black forests cried in their gloom, "Not here!" The river bowed and circled westward. Sullenly, silently, yet proudly, she swept into the western sea. As she swept she sang low minor melody; as she sang she scattered gold carelessly to the black children. But ere she died in the depth of the sea she gave to her strongest and blackest sons, Iron — the precious gift of Iron. They fashioned it cunningly and welded it in fairy forms and sent it to the ends of earth to make all men awake. And men awoke. They awoke on the cunning breast of the river's self and kingdom on kingdom arose until the empire of the Songhay rivaled the empires of the world. The sound of the might of Negro land echoed in Carthage and grew in Numidia and gave fairy tales to the Middle Sea.

Away to the south and eastward and below the Mountains of the Moon the third broad river heard her sisters hurrying seaward. North and westward they had gone but she turned to the eternal east. Golden she lifted up her golden hands and stretched to Ophir, Punt and Tarshish her long, lithe finger. Her voice rose mighty in song until with a million stars in her throat she dropped wild singing in the southern sea and shuddered to the vastness of its silence.

Her black children sat in mine, fortress, temple and flowering field and traded with dark traders beyond the India Sea, till lo: out of the north came a cry, a cry like the anguish of a soul. For back in the bowels of the land men heard the running of three rivers and rushed away madly; for they were those that would not hear and could not see. On they ran, on, on and eastward ringing their spears and crying their great, awful cry of war. As locusts swarming they passed the north of the glooming forest with its dim red faerie; eastward they looked upon the inland oceans and southward they sent their war cry reeling to the Mountains of the Moon.

There came a shouting in the wilderness and again as swarming bees onward they came, and again the war cry echoed to the stars. Over the ruin of things that were passed that black and human flood until its angry surf dashed into the vast, red Heart of the Land, and knew the haunted spell-cursed realm of the Last River. Mighty was this last of rivers — a river of rivers, an endless lacing and swirling and curling and swelling and streaming of wild, weird waters beneath the giant jungle, where the lion, the leopard and the elephant slept with the long, slim snake.

Hand in hand and voice to voice these waters whirled in one vast circle within the bosom of the land saying their incantations. They shouldered past the mountains and sang past all the seas, then shunning the glaring desert and in gathering themselves to one swarming flood they thrilled and thundered to the sea. Snake-like and lion strong they gathered the children, the little dark and weeping children, and lo, beyond on swelling waters rose a hoarse, harsh cry and slim and sail-like fingers beckoned to the westward deeps. The river paused and rose red and reeking in the sunlight — thundered to the sea — thundered through the sea in one long line of blood, with tossing limbs and the echoing cries of death and pain.

On, on! the bloody waters, with those pale ghost fingers of ship and sail, with gold and iron, hurt and hell, rolled, swelled and tumbled, until the laughing islands of the western sea grew dark and dumb with pain and in the world, the great new world a Sorrow was planted and the Sorrow grew.

1914 · vol 8

OF THE CHILDREN OF PEACE

Come, all my father's children, and sit beside my knee, here with this child of mine, and listen:

Have you ever seen a soldier? It is a brave sight, is it not? Once upon a time, many, many years before your dear little curly heads were born, I remember seeing an army that marched because a King was visiting an Emperor. Berlin was joy mad. Houses streamed with color and music reeled and rioted. Then came the army. Tall, handsome men, all gold and silver and broadcloth, sworded, spurred and plumed, led on horses that curvetted and tossed their shining bits. (Do you not love a horse with his great, sweet eyes and quivery, shining softness?) Next came the soldiers, erect, rigid, "Eyes left!" Pit-pat, pit-pat! Clasping their little innocent guns. Next came the artillery: files of wildly prancing horses dragging long leaden things. How the crowd roared. The King bowed to the Emperor and the Emperor bowed to the King, and there rose a great cry of pride and joy and battle from the people. With that cry I seemed suddenly to awake. I somehow saw *through;* (you know sometimes how you seem to see, but are blind until something happens and you really see?)

I saw then what I see now. I saw and see the WAR that men said could not be.

Gone was all the brave tinsel, the glitter, sheen and music. The men trudged and limped, naked and dirty, with sodden, angry, distorted faces; their eyes were sunken and bloodshot, with murder in them; they staggered over corpses and severed arms and feet and dead horses and they carried — not little innocent guns, but little innocent children; they dragged, not pale and leaden guns, but pale and bounden women, and before them staggered and crept old women and grandfathers, the sick and the maimed, the weak and the half-grown boys and girls.

I heard the cry that hovered over this fearsome army: it was a wail of hunger and crime, of thirst and pain and death, and the cry rose and met an answering cry that came from beyond the forest to the West.

Two toddling children slipped from their father's arms and met in the gloom of that forest, where the beasts cowered and livid, disbodied hands seemed to creep in the darkness.

"Mother," they whispered.

"Mama," they cried.

"*Mütterchen,*" they sobbed.

Wild with horror two bound mothers beat their naked hands against the gun carriages, groping and struggling through the gloom, as death flamed through their hearts.

Then the armies met. Two fathers leapt from the two armies ahead and each seized the other's child. They strangled and crushed and maimed and murdered it, till each baby lay pale, limp and dead.

(Nay, shrink not, my children; horrible as the tale may be, the truth is worse and you must know it.)

Then War was loose. Then six million human beings left their fields of golden grain and the busy hum of their factories and taking their own children for weapons dashed them against the trees and the lampposts and the churches and wallowed and gasped in their blood!

Come, all my father's children and hear how beyond the blue mists of the Everlasting Sea, the mothers mad with hunger, grief and pain, are fronting the blood-stained heavens with bared and haunted breasts and are shrieking:

"Why?"

"Why?"

Their shriek is the booming of guns, and the booming of cannon is the shriek of mothers.

And you must answer, Children of Peace, you must answer!

You must cry: "There is no why!"

"The cause of War is Preparation for War."

"The cause of Preparation for War is the Hatred and Despising of Men, your and my Brothers."

"War is murder in a red coat."

"War is raped mothers and bleeding fathers and strangled children."

"War is Death, Hate, Hunger and Pain!"

"Hell is War!"

And when you believe this with all your little hearts;

And when you cry it across the seas and across the years with all your little voices —

Then shall the Mothers of all dead Children hear;

Then shall the Sisters of all dead Brothers hear; then shall the Daughters of all dead Fathers hear; then shall the Women rise and say:

"War is done."

"Henceforward and forever there shall be no organized murder of men, for the children we bear shall be the Children of Peace, else there shall be no children."

Amen!

But cry, little Children, cry and cry loud and soon, for until you and the Mothers speak, the men of the world bend stupid and crazed beneath the burden of hate and death.

Behold, this old and awful world is but one slaughter-pen, one tale of innocent blood and senseless hate and strife.

Look yonder!

In the gloomy forest all is still, save here a red and flickering flame and there a last trembling sob. Only one living thing passes across the night: a horse — a gaunt, sweating horse, with bloody nostrils, great painstruck eyes, and bowels trailing on the earth. He hears his Emperor bugling "Victory!" to the King. Turning, he staggers toward him and whimpers as he goes.

1914 ~ vol 8

The Louisiana Historical Society has been celebrating the centennial of the Battle of New Orleans. Neighboring states were invited, the English Consul sent a gracious message, the Government sent a warship and the President sent a representative. There were white soldiers, white orators and white school children but the colored people had no part. Evidently the erudite association quite forgot that little speech which General Jackson made to his colored troops December 18, 1814:

To the Men of Color: Soldiers! From the shores of Mobile I collected you to arms; I invited you to share in the perils and to divide the glory of your white countrymen. I expected much from you, for I was not uninformed of those qualities which must render you so formidable to an invading foe. I knew that you could endure hunger and thirst and all the hardships of war. I knew that you loved the land of your nativity, and that, like ourselves, you had to defend all that is most dear to man. But you surpass my hopes. I have found in you, united to these qualities, that noble enthusiasm which impels to great deeds.

Soldiers! The President of the United States shall be informed of your conduct on the present occasion; and the voice of the representatives of the American nation shall applaud your valor, as your general now praises your ardor. The enemy is near. His sails cover the lakes. But the brave are united; and if he finds us contending among ourselves, it will be for the prize of valor and fame, its noblest reward.

1914 · vol 9

It seems fair to judge the christianity of white folk by two present day developments: the World War and Billy Sunday.* As to the widespread and costly murder being waged today by the children of the Prince of Peace comment is unnecessary. It simply spells christianity's failure.

As to Billy Sunday there is room for opinions. Personally we do not object to him; he is quite natural under the circumstances and a fit expression of his day. He is nearly the same thing as the whirling dervish, the snake dancer and devotee of Mumbo Jumbo. Such methods of appealing to primitive passions and emotions have been usual in the history of the world.

Today they are joined, in the case of Mr. Sunday, to picturesque abuse of the English language, unusual contortions and a curious moral obtuseness which allows Mr. Sunday to appropriate a whole speech belonging to Robert Ingersol** and use it as his own. The result has been a large number of converts and widespread demand for Mr. Sunday's services. All this seems necessary. Evidently Mr. Sunday's methods are the only ones that appeal to white Christians. Reason does not appeal. Suffering and poverty does not appeal. The lynching and burning of human beings and torturing of women has no effect. Yet the contortions of Mr. Sunday bring people down the "sawdust" trail.

Selah!

But hereafter let no white man sneer at the medicine men of West Africa or the howling of the Negro revival. The Negro church is at least democratic. It welcomes everybody. It draws no color-line.

1914 · vol 9

* Billy Sunday: Traveling tent evangelist in vogue in the U.S.A. during the First World War years
** Robert Ingersol: Agnostic and author

The Persistent Onslaught

The quiet insidious persistent attempt to keep the mass of the Negroes in America in just sufficient ignorance to render them incapable of realizing their power or resisting the position of inferiority into which the bulk of the nation is determined to thrust them was never stronger than today. Let us not be deceived.

It is true that our illiteracy has decreased enormously and that the number of our children reported to be in school is larger than ever before. At the same time our illiteracy has not decreased as quickly as it might have. . . .

As a race we are still kept in ignorance far below the average standard of this nation and of the present age, and the ideals set before our children in most cases are far below their possibilities and reasonable promise.

This is true not by accident but by design, and by the design not so much of the laboring white masses of the nation but rather by the design of rich and intelligent people, and particularly by those who masquerade as the Negroes' "friends." Their attack on real education for Negroes is in reality one with their attack on education for working men in general and this is part of the great modern attack upon democracy.

Of course, this movement masquerades as industrial and vocational training in an age which is preeminently industrial. It is thus difficult for the average colored man to descry its persistent and tremendous dangers to our ultimate survival as a race and as American citizens.

The Basic Injustice

No one denies that beneath the basic demand for industrial and vocational training lies a fundamental truth . . . It is the duty of all men to work and this work usually renders a service to the community for which the community is willing to pay with services and materials in return.

Nevertheless the average man must be trained for work which the average community will reward with a living wage. In these days of intricate technique such training cannot be acquired by chance or as a side issue or as an afterthought. It must form an integral part of every person's education.

"Therefore," says the principal of the school with the largest Negro attendance in Harlem, "I am going to train these Negroes as cooks and gardeners."

The Basic Fallacy

But wait; is work the object of life or is life the object of work? Are men to earn a living or simply to live for the sake of working? Is there any justice in making a particular body of men the drudges of society, destined for the worst work under the worst conditions and at the lowest pay, simply because a majority of their fellow men for more or less indefinite and superficial reasons do not like them?

Manifestly life, and abundant life, is the object of industry and we teach men to earn a living in order that their industry may administer to their own lives and the lives of their fellows. If, therefore, any human being has large ability it is not only for his advantage but for the advantage of all society that he be put to the work that he can do best. To assume that ability is to be measured by so-called racial characteristics — by color, by hair or by stature — is not only ridiculous but dangerous. . . .

While we teach men to earn a living, that teaching is incidental and subordinate to the larger training of intelligence in human beings and to the largest development of self-realization in men. Those who would deny this to the Negro race are enemies of mankind.

The Result

The result of limiting the education of Negroes under the mask of fitting them for work is the slow strangulation of the Negro college.

None of the five major Negro colleges has today any solid financial prospect for growth and development. Not only that but they are regularly sneered at by men who dare not raise their arguments above a sneer. We hear again and again the usual lie that these colleges are persisting in the curriculum of fifty years ago. As a matter of fact nearly all of them conform to the standard of education as laid down by the highest authorities in this country.

What they are really asked to do is to adopt a course of study which does not conform to modern standards, which no modern system of education will recognize and which condemns the student who takes it to end his education in a blind alley. It is the unforgivable sin of some of the greatest so-called industrial schools that the boy who is induced to take their course is absolutely unfitted thereby from continuing his education at a recognized modern institution. This is a crime against childhood for which any nation ought to be ashamed.

Do Negroes oppose this because they are ashamed of having their children trained to work? Certainly not. But they know that if their children are compelled to cook and sew when they ought to be learning to read, write and cipher, they will not be able to enter the high school or go to college as the white children are doing. It is a deliberate, despicable attempt to throttle the Negro child before he knows enough to protest.

The Excuse

Even in industrial training the white authorities are persistently dishonest. They will not train our children in good paying trades and respectable vocations. They want them to be servants and menials. The excuse which is continually brought forward, particularly in the North, is that there is "no opening" for them in the higher ranges of the industrial world! For this reason opportunities for the best industrial training are persistently denied colored students.

Trade schools in many of the large cities have the habit of forcing colored students who apply into the courses for domestic service or sewing on the plea that millinery, carpentry and various lines of mechanical work offer no opportunity for colored folk. Surely this reduces the argument for industrial training to rank absurdity and the cause of real, honest industrial training deserves more sensible treatment than this.

Our Attitude

In all these arguments and actions there blazes one great and shining light: the persistent army of Negro boys and girls pushing through high school and college continues to increase. Negro mothers and fathers are not being entirely deceived. They know that intelligence and self-development are the only means by which the Negro is to win his way in the modern world. They persist in pushing their children on through the highest courses. May they always continue to do so; and may the Negro students in the coming years resist the contemptible temptation so persistently laid before this race to train its children simply as menials and scavengers.

1914 · vol 10

BOOKER T. WASHINGTON

The death of Mr. Washington marks an epoch in the history of America. He was the greatest Negro leader since Frederick Douglass, and the most distinguished man, white or black, who has come out of the South since the Civil War. His fame was international and his influence far-reaching. Of the good that he accomplished there can be no doubt: he directed the attention of the Negro race in America to the pressing necessity of economic development; he emphasized technical education and he did much to pave the way for an understanding between the white and darker races.

On the other hand there can be no doubt of Mr. Washington's mistakes and shortcomings: he never adequately grasped the growing bond of politics and industry; he did not understand the deeper foundations of human training and his basis of better understanding between white and black was founded on caste.

We may then generously and with deep earnestness lay on the grave of Booker T. Washington testimony of our thankfulness for his undoubted help in the accumulation of Negro land and property, his establishment of Tuskegee and spreading of industrial education and his compelling of the white South to at least think of the Negro as a possible man.

On the other hand, in stern justice, we must lay on the soul of this man, a heavy responsibility for the consummation of Negro disfranchisement, the decline of the Negro college and public school and the firmer establishment of color caste in this land.

What is done is done. This is no fit time for recrimination or complaint. Gravely and with bowed head let us receive what this great figure gave of good, silently rejecting all else. Firmly and unfalteringly let the Negro race in America, in bleeding Haiti and throughout the world close ranks and march steadily on, determined as never before to work and save and endure, but never to swerve from their great goal: the right to vote, the right to know, and the right to stand as men among men throughout the world.

It is rumored that Mr. Washington's successor at

Tuskegee will be Robert Russa Moton, Commandant of Cadets at Hampton. If this proves true Major Moton will enter on his new duties with the sympathy and good will of his many friends both black and white.

1915 · vol 11

SIR ROGER CASEMENT — PATRIOT, MARTYR

Sir Roger Casement is dead. He has been put to death by the English Government on the charge of treason. His crime was this: He headed a rebellion of the Irish against the English and negotiated with the Germans for help. Just before the outbreak of the rebellion, Easter week, a German steamship laden with arms went to the coast of Ireland accompanied by a submarine with Casement on board. He was arrested on landing, tried, condemned and sentenced to death. Thus England has muddled into one more blunder in her stupid list of blunders in dealing with Ireland.

Traitor is a hard word and Sir Roger Casement as the world's hard and fast laws have it was a traitor to his country, England. But let us look into this man's life and see if it is really possible to reconcile his antecedents and his character with the stigma of treason.

His friends, and they are many and influential — Galsworthy,* G. K. Chesterton, Israel Zangwill, Sir Henry Nevinson were among them — speak of him as being "generous, sympathetic and sincere." *Sincere*, mark you!

He rendered England a long consular service extending almost without interruption from 1895 to 1913. It seems to have been spent in all sorts of out-of-the-way places: the Portuguese provinces of Angola and the cocoa islands of San Thomé and Principe, the Congo and in South

* John Galsworthy, G. K. Chesterton, Israel Zangwill: British authors

America. It was he who, on reading Sir Henry Nevinson's report of the Congo atrocities, said that the report in all its horrors was still not horrible and revolting enough and it was he who later on opened the eyes of the world to the scandal of the rubber trade on the Putumayo in South America. . . .

All the impressionable, vigorous years of his manhood, you see, were spent in witnessing acts of oppression and lawlessness and in efforts to offset those acts. He became "obsessed" with a horror at the "frightfulness" which those in great places wreak upon those in small.

Last of all he came home to see his country, his dear native land, Ireland, still bleeding and languishing in the hands of her historic oppressor. Just how far the attitude of the other members of Sinn Fein was absolutely sincere we are not prepared to say; so far as Sir Roger Casement is concerned there can be almost no doubt but that he believed in Germany as the deliverer of Ireland from England's cruelty. To him Ireland — not England — was the land to which he owed allegiance. We can but judge a man by his beliefs.

And so he died an Irish patriot whose memory will be cherished at every Irish fireside as one who died for his country. As Sir Henry Nevinson succinctly puts it: "We (the English) execute a worthless rebel and for Ireland a heroic saint emerges from the felon's grave." This was the time for English expediency rather than the bleak upholding of laws and customs. Someone has blundered.

1916 · vol 12

THE BATTLE OF EUROPE

The war is still with us, has almost become a commonplace, and yet there is no thinking man who does not send his mind two years back and remember the assurance with which he said in those bewildering, tumultuous days of August, 1914, "This cannot last, we are too civilized."

Well, civilization has met its Waterloo. We have read of attacks by gas, of raids on non-fortified towns, of Zeppelins dropping bombs on women and children, and the whole campaign of "frightfulness" which left us at first cold and faint and even yet inspires in us a sick distaste. What good can come out of it all? Much is still on the knees of the gods; but it takes no prophet to presage the advent of many things — notably the greater emancipation of European women, the downfall of monarchies, the gradual but certain dissolution of caste and the advance of a true Socialism. All this and much more. But for the present, especially for us, there is coming a gradual and subtle encouragement to strengthen race predilections and revel in them unashamed.

The civilization by which America insists on measuring us and to which we must conform our natural tastes and inclinations is the daughter of that European civilization which is now rushing furiously to its doom. This civilization with its aeroplanes and submarines, its wireless and its "big business" is no more static than that of those other civilizations in the rarest days of Greece and Rome. Behind all this gloss of culture and wealth and religion has been lurking the world-old lust for bloodshed and power gained at the cost of honor.

The realization of all this means for us the reassembling of old ideals. Honor which has had no meaning for us in this land of inconstant laws, takes on a new aspect; mediocrity, so long as it does not mean degradation, is sweet; peace — not "at any price" — is a precious boon; old standards of beauty beckon us again, not the blue-eyed, white-skinned types which are set before us in school and literature but rich, brown and black men and women with glowing dark eyes and crinkling hair. Music has always been ours; but with the disappearance of those *effete* ideals comes the assurance that the plantation song is more in unison with the "harmony of the spheres" than Wagner's greatest triumph. Life, which in this cold Occident stretched in bleak, conventional lines before us, takes on a warm, golden hue that harks back to the heritage of Africa and the tropics.

Brothers, the war has shown us the cruelty of the civilization of the West. History has taught us the futility of the civilization of the East. Let ours be the civilization of no *man*, but of *all men*.

This is the truth that sets us free.

1916 · vol 12

CONSOLATION

Colored folk can always get a dubious sort of consolation in knowing that they have not always had a monopoly of the attentions of the discourteous and the cruel. At a recent dinner given to the oldest woman doctor in the United States, Dr. Anna Manning Comfort told of the indignities which she suffered at Bellevue Hospital in 1865 for the unforgivable crime of being female: "We had to go to Bellevue Hospital for our practical work, and the indignities we were made to suffer are beyond belief. There were five hundred young men students taking postgraduate courses; we were jeered at and catcalled, and the 'old war horses,' the doctors, joined the younger men.

"We were considered aggressive. They said women did not have the same brains as men and were not trustworthy. All the work at the hospital was made as repulsively unpleasant for us as possible. There were originally six in the class, but all but two were unable to put up with the treatment to which we were subjected and dropped out. I trembled whenever I went to the hospital, and I said once that I could not bear it. Finally the women went to the authorities who said that if we were not respectfully treated they would take the charter from the hospital.

"As a physician there was nothing that I could do that satisfied people. If I wore square-toed shoes and swung my arms they said I was mannish, and if I carried a parasol and wore a ribbon in my hair they said I was too feminine. If I smiled they said I had too much levity, and if I sighed they said I had no sand.

"They tore down my sign when I began to practice; the drug stores did not like to fill my prescriptions, and the older doctors would not consult with me. But that little band of women made it possible for the other women who have come later into the field to do their work. When my first patients came and saw me they said I was too young, and they asked in horrified tones if I had studied dissecting just like the men. They were shocked at that, but they were more shocked when my bills were sent in to find that I charged as much as a man."

Remember this is the story of the treatment of a white woman by chivalrous American white men, the same men who tremble with indignation lest a black man look at one of these "beautiful" creatures.

1916 · vol 12

THE DRAMA AMONG BLACK FOLK

Hear ye, hear ye! Men of all the Americas, and listen to the tale of the Eldest and Strongest of the Races of men whose faces be Black. Hear ye, hear ye! For lo! Upon this night a world shall pass before your souls, bathed in color, wound with song and set to the dancing of a thousand feet. And this shall be the message of this pageantry: Of the Black man's Gift of Iron to the world; of Ethiopia and her Glory; of the Valley of Humiliation through which God would she pass and of the Vision Everlasting when the Cross of Christ and the Star of Freedom set atop the Pillar of Eternal Light. Men of the world keep silence and in reverence see this holy thing.

This has been the opening cry of the dark and crimson-turbaned Herald in three presentations of the pageant, "The Star of Ethiopia," given by colored people in New York, Washington and Philadelphia before audiences aggregating nearly 35,000 people.

The last of these three pageants was given in Philadelphia during the month of May before audiences of eight thousand. It was in many respects the most perfect of the pageants. For while it lacked the curious thrill and newness of the New York production and the mysterious glamour of shadow, star and sky which made the Washington pageant unforgettable, yet Philadelphia in its smoothness and finish was technically the best. As this last production represents possibly the end of the series it is a fitting time to review this effort.

The Negro is essentially dramatic. His greatest gift to the world has been and will be a gift of art, of appreciation and realization of beauty. Such was his gift to Egypt, even as the dark Herald cried in the second scene of the pageant:

Hear ye, hear ye! All them that come to know the truth and listen to the tale of the Wisest and Gentlest of the Races of Men whose faces be Black. Hear ye, hear ye! And learn the ancient Glory of Ethiopia, All-Mother of men, whose wonders men forgot. See how beneath the Mountains of the Moon, alike in the Valley of Father Nile and in ancient Negro-land and Atlantis the Black Race ruled and strove and fought and sought the Star of Faith and Freedom even as other races did and do. Fathers of Men and Sires of Children golden, black and brown, keep silence and hear this mighty word.

All through Africa, pageantry and dramatic recital is close mingled with religious rites and in America the "Shout" of the church revival is in its essential pure drama. The American Negro early turned toward the theatre. Ira Aldridge, their first great actor, was born in Maryland in

1810 and educated in Glasgow. He became before his death the first of European tragedians, honored and decorated by nearly every European government. There was, of course, no career for him in America. Here by the unbending law of exclusion Negro minstrelsy developed first with white men and then with colored actors.

In later days Cole and Johnson and Williams and Walker lifted minstrelsy by sheer force of genius into the beginning of a new drama. White people refused to support the finest of their new conceptions like the "Red Moon" and the cycle apparently stopped. Recently, however, with the growth of a considerable number of colored theatres and moving picture places, a new and inner demand for Negro drama has arisen which is only partially satisfied by the vaudeville actors. Today in Harlem it is being curiously supplied by setting companies of colored actors to playing recent Broadway successess. . . . The next step will undoubtedly be the slow growth of a new folk drama built around the actual experience of Negro American life.

Already there are beginnings here and there, but especially in Washington, where Angelina Grimké's* strong play, "Rachel," was produced last year.

I seemed to see this development some years ago, and as a kind of beginning I sketched the pageant, the "Star of Ethiopia," in 1911. It was not staged until 1913 at the Emancipation Exposition in New York City. There it was made a part of the Exposition and attempted with three hundred and fifty colored actors. I can feel again the strain of that first attempt and the sound of the voice of the Herald crying:

Hear ye, hear ye! Eternal Children of the Lord, ye little ones within whose veins the blood of Ethiopia flows and

* Angelina E. Grimké and her sister Sarah, famous women abolitionists from South Carolina

flames. Hear ye, hear ye! And listen to the tale of the Humblest and Mightiest of the Races of Men whose faces be Black. Behold the Star of Faith so nearly lost, yet found again and placed against high heaven through the crucifixion of God and little children. Sons and Daughters of Men keep silence and hear this beautiful thing.

This first pageant was in audience and acting a great success. "An impressive spectacle," as the *Outlook* said, "both from a historical point of view and as a forecast."

Then came my dream. It seemed to me that it might be possible with such a demonstration to get people interested in this development of Negro drama to teach on the one hand the colored people themselves the meaning of their history and their rich, emotional life through a new theatre, and on the other, to reveal the Negro to the white world as a human, feeling being.

I started out to raise three thousand dollars. By contributing five hundred myself and by the wonderful gift of one young woman I succeeded in raising a little over two thousand dollars in cash; my other pledges failed. With this money the Washington pageant was given in the open air with twelve hundred colored participants. It was a wonderful thing.

But with all this it was financially a partial failure and I found myself at the end with my capital reduced one-half. Yet I looked upon it simply as a certain, mild Valley of Humiliation repeating to myself the words of the Herald at the beginning of the fourth scene:

Hear ye, hear ye! All ye that come to see the light and listen to the tale of the Bravest and Truest of the Races of Men whose faces be Black! Hear ye, hear ye! And learn how men of Negro blood did suffer the Pains of Death and the Humiliation of Hell, yet did not die. Listen, Mothers of Men and Daughters of Almighty God beneath whose hearts these dark and beautiful children lie and have lain buried — listen and hear this awful thing.

I determined to make one more effort at Philadelphia. Here in celebration of the One Hundredth General Conference of the African M. E. Church the pageant was given the third and perhaps the last time with one thousand and seventy-eight colored actors. It was to all who saw it a Vision Everlasting like to the Herald's cry before the impressive scene:

Hear ye, hear ye! All them that dwell by the Rivers of Waters and in the beautiful, the Valley of Shadows, and listen to the ending of this tale. Learn, Sisters and Brothers, how above the Fear of God, Labor doth build on Knowledge; how Justice tempers Science and how Beauty shall be crowned in Love beneath the Cross. Listen, O Isles, for all the pageant returns in dance and song to build this Tower of Eternal Light beneath the Star. Keep silence and let your souls sing with this last and latest word.

And so it ended beautifully and full of satisfaction, due in greatest measure to the genius and devotion of Charles Burroughs, Dora Cole Norman, Richard Brown and Augustus Dill, my chief helpers, and to hundreds of others. And yet, alas, the whole of my little capital is swept away except a thousand dollars inextricably tied up in costumes and properties. What now is the next step? Already there are faint signs: A Shakespeare pageant in Washington and two masques in Cincinnati. Numerous inquiries from elsewhere have come.

The great fact has been demonstrated that pageantry among colored people is not only possible, but in many ways of unsurpassed beauty and can be made a means of uplift and education and the beginning of a folk drama. On the other hand, the white public has shown little or no interest in the movement. The American Pageant Association has been silent, if not actually contemptuous, and there have been within my own race the usual petty but hurting insinuations of personal greed and selfishness as the real incentives behind my efforts. Unless, therefore, from unforeseen and unknown sources I receive help and encouragement I shall lay this effort down and bequeath it to new hands crying with the last cry of my Herald:

Hear ye, hear ye! All them that sing before the Lord and forget not the Vision of the Eldest and Strongest of the Races of Men whose faces be Black. Hear ye, hear ye! And remember forever and one day the Star of Ethiopia, All-Mother of Men, who gave the world the Iron Gift and Gift of Faith, the Pain of Humility and Sorrow Song of Pain, and Freedom, Eternal Freedom, underneath the Star. Arise and go, Children of Philadelphia — the Play is done — the Play is done.

1916 · vol 12

ATLANTA

Atlanta sits on Seven Hills, but the people who have made blood money out of Coca-Cola have added an eighth, Druid Hill: a modern suburb done modernwise. The Atlanta rich have wrung city taxes out of poor blacks and poor whites and then squandered wealth to lay mile on mile of beautiful boulevard through silent and empty forests with mile on mile of nine-inch water mains and sewers of latest design, while here and there rise grudgingly the spreading castles of the Sudden Rich; but in the city's heart, in the ruts of the Seven Hills, the children sicken and die, because there is no city water, and five thousand black children sit in the streets, for there are no seats in the schools. Only a single new colored schoolhouse for thirty years, no colored library, but on the portal of the white library, donated by millionaire Andrew Carnegie, this speaking inscription:

Aesop, Homer, Virgil, Carnegie, Dante, Milton, Poe.

Yet the young men of Atlanta are strong; the whites are strong and blatant, but the blacks are strong and silent; college-bred, clean-cut, unflinching; their college club is now the only "university club" in the city, for the white club died with the crucifixion of Leo Frank.*

1917 · vol 13

VOTES FOR WOMEN

Some 75,000 Negro voters in the State of New York will be asked to decide this month as to whether or not they are willing that women should have the vote in this State. It is an unpleasant but well-known fact that hitherto American Negro voters have, in the majority of cases, not been favorable to woman suffrage. This attitude has been taken for two main reasons:

First, the Negro, still imbued by the ideals of a past generation, does not realize the new status of women in industrial and social life. Despite the fact that within his own group women are achieving economic independence even faster than whites, he thinks of these as exceptional and abnormal and looks forward to the time when his wages will be large enough to support his wife and daughters in comparative idleness at home.

Secondly, the American Negro is particularly bitter at the attitude of many white women: at the naive assumption that the height of his ambition is to marry them, at their artificially inspired fear of every dark face, which leads to frightful accusations and suspicions, and at their sometimes insulting behavior toward him in public places.

Notwithstanding the undoubted weight of these two reasons, the American Negro must remember:

* Leo Frank: A Jewish school teacher, lynched in 1916 in Atlanta, Georgia, in a wave of anti-Semitism

First, that the day when women can be considered as the mere appendages of men, dependent upon their bounty and educated chiefly for their pleasure, has gone by; that as an intelligent, self-supporting human being a woman has just as good a right to a voice in her own government as has any man; and that the denial of this right is as unjust as is the denial of the right to vote to American Negroes.

Secondly, two wrongs never made a right. We cannot punish the insolence of certain classes of American white women or correct their ridiculous fears by denying them their undoubted rights.

It goes without saying that the women's vote, particularly in the South, will be cast almost unanimously, at first, for every reactionary Negro-hating piece of legislation that is proposed; that the Bourbons and the demagogs, who are today sitting in the National Legislature by the reason of stolen votes, will have additional backing for some years from the votes of white women.

But against this consideration it must be remembered that these same women are going to learn political justice a great deal more quickly than did their men and that despite their prejudices their very emergence into the real, hard facts of life and out of the silly fairyland to which their Southern male masters beguile them is going to teach them sense in time.

Moreover, it is going to be more difficult to disfranchise colored women in the South than it was to disfranchise colored men. Even southern "gentlemen," as used as they are to the mistreatment of colored women, cannot in the blaze of present publicity physically beat them away from the polls. Their economic power over them will be smaller than their power over the men and while you can still bribe some pauperized Negro laborers with a few dollars at election time, you cannot bribe Negro women.

It is, therefore, of the utmost importance that every single black voter in the State of New York should this month cast his ballot in favor of woman suffrage and that every black voter in the United States should do the same thing whenever and as often as he has opportunity.

It is only in such broad-minded willingness to do justice to all, even to his own temporary hurt, that the black man can prove his right not only to share, but to help direct modern culture.

1917 · vol 15

THE BLACK MAN AND THE UNIONS

I am among the few colored men who have tried conscientiously to bring about understanding and co-operation between American Negroes and the Labor Unions. I have sought to look upon the Sons of Freedom as simply a part of the great mass of the earth's Disinherited, and to realize that world movements which have lifted the lowly in the past and are opening the gates of opportunity to them today are of equal value for all men, white and black, then and now.

I carry on the title page, for instance, of this magazine the Union label, and yet I know, and every one of my Negro readers knows, that the very fact that this label is there is an advertisement that no Negro's hand is engaged in the printing of this magazine, since the International Typographical Union systematically and deliberately excludes every Negro that it dares from membership, no matter what his qualifications.

Even here, however, and beyond the hurt of mine own, I have always striven to recognize the real cogency of the Union argument. Collective bargaining has, undoubtedly, raised modern labor from something like chattel slavery to the threshold of industrial freedom, and in this advance of labor white and black have shared.

I have tried, therefore, to see a vision of vast union between the laboring forces, particularly in the South, and hoped for no distant day when the black laborer and the white laborer, instead of being used against each other as helpless pawns, should unite to bring real democracy in the South.

On the other hand, the whole scheme of settling the Negro problem, inaugurated by philanthropists and carried out during the last twenty years, has been based upon the idea of playing off black workers against white. That it is essentially a mischievous and dangerous program no sane thinker can deny, but it is peculiarly disheartening to realize that it is the Labor Unions themselves that have given this movement its greatest impulse and that today, at last, in East St. Louis have brought the most unwilling of us to acknowledge that in the present Union movement, as represented by the American Federation of Labor, there is absolutely no hope of justice for an American of Negro descent.

Personally, I have come to this decision reluctantly and in the past have written and spoken little of the closed door of opportunity, shut impudently in the faces of black men by organized white workingmen. I realize that by heredity and century-long lack of opportunity one cannot expect in the laborer that larger sense of justice and duty which we ought to demand of the privileged classes. I have, therefore, inveighed against color discrimination by employers and by the rich and well-to-do, knowing at the same time in silence that it is practically impossible for any colored man or woman to become a boiler maker or book binder, an electrical worker or glass maker, a worker in jewelry or leather, a machinist or metal polisher, a paper maker or piano builder, a plumber or a potter, a printer or a pressman, a telegrapher or a railway trackman, an electrotyper or stove mounter, a textile worker or tile layer, a trunk maker, upholsterer, carpenter, locomotive engineer, switchman, stone cutter, baker, blacksmith, boot and shoemaker, tailor, or any of a dozen other important well-paid employments, without encountering the open determination and unscrupulous opposition of the whole united labor movement of America. That further than this, if he should want to become a painter, mason, carpenter, plasterer, brickmaker or fireman he would be subject to humiliating discriminations by his fellow Union workers and be deprived of work at every possible opportunity, even in defiance of their own Union laws.

If, braving this outrageous attitude of the Unions, he succeeds in some small establishment or at some exceptional time at gaining employment, he must be labeled as a "scab" throughout the length and breadth of the land and written down as one who, for his selfish advantage, seeks to overthrow the labor uplift of a century.

1918 · vol 15

THE BLACK SOLDIER

This number of *The Crisis* is dedicated, first, to the nearly 100,000 men of Negro descent who are today called to arms for the United States. It is dedicated, also, to the million dark men of Africa and India, who have served in the armies of Great Britain, and to the equal, if not larger, number who are fighting for France and the other Allies.

To these men we want to say above all: Have courage and determination. You are not fighting simply for Europe; you are fighting for the world, and you and your people are a part of the world.

This war is an End and, also, a Beginning. Never again will darker people of the world occupy just the place they had before. Out of this war will rise, soon or late, an independent China; a self-governing India, and Egypt with representative institutions; an Africa for the Africans, and not merely for business exploitation. Out of this war will rise, too, an American Negro, with the right to vote and the right to work and the right to live without insult. These things may not and will not come at once; but they are written in the stars. . . .

1918 · vol 16

PEACE

The nightmare is over. The world awakes. The long, horrible years of dreadful night are passed. Behold the sun! We have dreamed. Frightfully have we dreamed unimagined, unforgettable things — all lashed with blood and tears. Bound and damned we writhed and could not stir. The contortions of our hated souls stifled our hunted bodies. We were cold and numb and deaf and blind, and yet the air was visioned with the angels of Hell; the earth was a vast groan; the sea was a festering sore, and we were flame.

And now suddenly we awake! It is done. We are sane. We are alive. Behold the Heavens and its stars; and this blood — this warm and dripping blood from our mad self-laceration — What of it? Can we not staunch it? Will we not? Hail, then, Holy Christmas time, Nineteen Hundred and Eighteen Years after the Birth, and five since the last Crucifixion.

On Earth, Peace, Good Will Toward Men.

1918 · vol 17

PAN-AFRICA

Europe had begun to look with covetous eyes toward Africa as early as 1415 when the Portuguese at the Battle of Ceuta gained a foothold in Morocco. Thereafter Prince Henry of Portugal instituted the series of explorations which resulted not only in the discovery of Cape Verde, the Guinea Coast and the Cape of Good Hope, but by 1487 gave to Portugal the possession of a very fair slice of the African East Coast. This was the beginning of the Portuguese Colonies of Guinea, Angola and East Africa. Other European nations, France, Holland, Spain, England and Denmark, followed and set up trading stations along the African coast whose chief reason for existence was the fostering of the slave trade.

But the partition of Africa as we know it is much more recent and begins with the founding in 1884 of the Congo Free State whose inception was so zealously fostered by Leopold of Belgium and which in 1908 was annexed to Belgium. The "scramble" for African colonies was on and within a quarter of a century Africa was virtually in the hands of Europe.

In this division the British Empire gained a network of possessions extending from the Anglo-Egyptian Sudan down to South Africa with valuable holdings on the East Coast and in Somaliland. France came next with an actually larger area, but with a smaller population. Her spoils reached from Morocco and Algeria, including the Algerian Sahara, to the French Congo, and on the Eastern Coast comprised Madagascar and French Somaliland. Germany, who was late in entering the game of colonization, contrived none the less to become mistress of four very valuable colonies, Togoland, Kamerun, South-West Africa and East Africa. Italy's and Spain's possessions were relatively unimportant, embracing for the former,

Eritrea and Italian Somaliland, and for the latter Rio de Oro and the Muni River settlements.

This was the state of affairs when the war broke out in 1914. In Africa the only independent states were the Republic of Liberia, and the kingdom of Abyssinia which, according to history, has been independent since the days of Menelek, the reputed son of Solomon and the Queen of Sheba. The number of souls thus under the rule of aliens, in the case of England, France, Germany and Belgium, amounted to more than 110 000,000. During the course of the war Germany lost all four of her African colonies with a population estimated at 13,420,000. It is the question of the reapportionment of this vast number of human beings which has started the Pan-African movement. Colored America is indeed involved.

> *If we do not feel the chain*
> *When it works another's pain,*
> *Are we not base slaves indeed*
> *Slaves unworthy to be freed?*

Colonial Imperialism in Africa

The suggestion was made that these colonies which Germany lost should not be handed over to any other nation of Europe but should, under the guidance of *organized civilization*, be brought to a point of development which shall finally result in autonomous states. This plan met with criticism and ridicule. Let the natives develop along their own lines and they will "go back," has been the cry. Back to what, in Heaven's name?

Is a civilization naturally backward because it is different? Outside of cannibalism, which can be matched in this country, at least, by lynching, there is no vice and no degradation in native African customs which can begin to touch the horrors thrust upon them by white masters.

Drunkenness, terrible diseases, immorality, all these things have been the gifts of European civilization. There is no need to dwell on German and Belgian atrocities, the world knows them too well. Nor have France and England been blameless. But even supposing that these masters had been models of kindness and rectitude, who shall say that any civilization is in itself so superior that it must be superimposed upon another nation without the expressed and intelligent consent of the people most concerned. The culture indigenous to a country, its folk-customs, its art, all this must have free scope or there is no such thing as freedom for the world.

The truth is, white men are merely juggling with words — or worse — when they declare that the withdrawal of Europeans from Africa would plunge that continent into chaos.

What Europe, and indeed only a small group in Europe, wants in Africa is not a field for the spread of European civilization, but a field for exploitation. They covet the raw materials — ivory, diamonds, copper and rubber in which the land abounds, and even more do they covet cheap native labor to mine and produce these things. Greed, naked, pitiless lust for wealth and power, lie back of all of Europe's interest in Africa and the white world knows it and is not ashamed.

Any readjustment of Africa is not fair and cannot be lasting which does not consider the interests of native Africans and peoples of African descent. Prejudice, in European colonies in Africa, against the ambitious Negro is greater than in America, and that is saying much.

But with the establishment of a form of government which shall be based on the concept that Africa is for Africans, there would be a chance for the colored American to emigrate and to go as a pioneer to a country which must, sentimentally at least, possess for him the same fascination as England does for Indian-born Englishmen.

This is not a "separatist" movement. There is no need to think that those who advocate the opening up of Africa for Africans and those of African descent desire to deport colored Americans to a foreign land. Once for all, let us realize that we are Americans, that we were brought here with the earliest settlers, and that the very sort of civilization from which we came made the complete adoption of western modes and customs imperative if we were to survive at all. In brief, there is nothing so indigenous, so completely "made in America" as we. It is as absurd to talk of a return to Africa, merely because that was our home 300 years ago, as it would be to expect the members of the Caucasian race to return to the fastnesses of the Caucasus Mountains from which, it is reputed, they sprang.

But it is true that we as a people are not given to colonization, and that thereby a number of essential occupations and interests have been closed to us which the redemption of Africa would open up. To help bear the burden of Africa does not mean any lessening of effort in our own problem at home. Rather it means increased interest. For any ebullition of action and feeling that results in an amelioration of the lot of Africa tends to ameliorate the condition of colored peoples throughout the world. And no man liveth to himself.

1919 · vol 17

FOR WHAT?

My God! For what am I thankful this night? For nothing. For nothing but the most commonplace of commonplaces: a table of gentlewomen and gentlemen — soft-spoken, sweet-tempered, full of human sympathy, who made me, a stranger, one of them.

Ours was a fellowship of common books, common

knowledge, mighty aims. We could laugh and joke and think as friends — and the *Thing* — the hateful, murderous, dirty *Thing* which in America we call "nigger-hatred" was not only not there — it could not even be understood. It was a curious monstrosity at which civilized folk laughed or looked puzzled.

There was no elegant and elaborate condescension of — "We once had a colored servant" — "My father was an Abolitionist" — "I've always been interested in *your people*" — there was only the community of kindred souls, the delicate reference for the Thought that led, the quick deference to the guests you left in quiet regret, knowing they were not discussing you behind your back with lies and license. God! It was simply human decency and I had to be thankful for it because I am an American Negro and white America, with saving exceptions, is cruel to everything that has black blood — and this was Paris, in the year of salvation, 1919.

Fellow blacks, we must join the democracy of Europe.

1919 · vol 17

THE FIELDS OF BATTLES

I have seen the wounds of France — the entrails of Rheims and the guts of Verdun, with their bare bones thrown naked to the insulting skies; villages in dust and ashes — villages that lay so low that they left no mark beneath the snow-swept landscape; walls that stood in wrecked and awful silence; rivers flowed and skies gleamed, but the trees, the land, the people were scarred and broken. Ditches darted hither and thither and wire twisted, barbed and poled, cloistered in curious, illogical places. Graves there were — everywhere and a certain breathless horror, broken by plodding soldiers and fugitive peasants.

We were at Château-Thierry in a room where the

shrapnel had broken across the dining-table and torn a mirror and wrecked a wall; then we hastened to Rheims, that riven city where scarce a house escaped its scar and the House of Houses stood, with its laced stone and empty, piteous beauty, high and broad, about the scattered death.

Then on we flew past silence and silent, broken walls to the black ridge that writhes northward like a vast grave. Its trees, like its dead, are young — broken and bent with fiery surprise — here the earth is ploughed angrily, there rise huts and blankets of wattles to hide the ways, and yonder in a hollow the Germans had built for years — concrete bungalows with electric lights, a bath-room for a Prince, and trenches and tunnels. Wide ways with German names ran in straight avenues through the trees and everywhere giant engines of death had sown the earth and cut the trees with iron.

Down again we went to the hungry towns behind the lines and up again to Verdun — the ancient fortress, with its ancient hills, where fort on fort had thundered four dream-dead years and on the plains between villages had sunk into the silent earth. The walls and moat hung gravely black and still, the city rose in clustered, drunken ruin here and in yellow ashes there, and in the narrow streets I saw my colored boys working for France.

On, on out of the destruction and the tears, down by bewildered Commercy and old Toul, where a great truck hurrying food to the starving nearly put our auto in a ditch, and up to Pont-à-Mousson where Joan of Arc on her great hill overlooks the hills of mighty Metz; then to Nancy and by the dark and winding Moselle to the snow-covered Vosges.

In yonder forest, day on day the Negro troops were held in leash. Then slowly they advanced, swinging a vast circle — down a valley and up again, with the singing of shells. I stood by their trenches, wattled and boarded, and saw where they rushed "over the top" to the crest, and looked on the field before Metz. Innocent it looked, but the barbed wire, thick and tough, belted it like heavy bushes and huddled in hollows lay the machine guns, nested in concrete walls, three feet thick, squatting low on the underbrush and scattering sputtering death up that silent hillside. Such wire! Such walls! How long the great, cradling sweep of land down the valley and over the German trenches to the village beyond, beside the silent, dark Moselle!

On by the river we went to the snow-covered Vosges, where beneath the shoulder of a mountain the Ninety-second Division held a sector, with quiet death running down at intervals. The trenches circled the hills, and dugouts nestled beneath by the battered villages.

We flew back by the hungry zone in the backwash of war — by Epinal and Domremy — Bourbonne-les-Bains and Chaumont and so — home to Paris.

1919 · vol 17

RETURNING SOLDIERS

We are returning from war! *The Crisis* and tens of thousands of black men were drafted into a great struggle. For bleeding France and what she means and has meant and will mean to us and humanity and against the threat of German race arrogance, we fought gladly and to the last drop of blood; for America and her highest ideals, we fought in far-off hope; for the dominant southern oligarchy entrenched in Washington, we fought in bitter resignation. For the America that represents and gloats in lynching, disfranchisement, caste, brutality and devilish insult — for this, in the hateful upturning and mixing of things, we were forced by vindictive fate to fight, also.

But today we return! We return from the slavery of uniform which the world's madness demanded us to don to the freedom of civil garb. We stand again to look America squarely in the face and call a spade a spade. We sing:

This country of ours, despite all its better souls have done and dreamed, is yet a shameful land.

It *lynches*.

And lynching is barbarism of a degree of contemptible nastiness unparalleled in human history. Yet for fifty years we have lynched two Negroes a week, and we have kept this up right through the war.

It *disfranchises* its own citizens.

Disfranchisement is the deliberate theft and robbery of the only protection of poor against rich and black against white. The land that disfranchises its citizens and calls itself a democracy lies and knows it lies.

It encourages *ignorance*.

It has never really tried to educate the Negro. A dominant minority does not want Negroes educated. It wants servants, dogs, whores and monkeys. And when this land allows a reactionary group by its stolen political power to force as many black folk into these categories as it possibly can, it cries in contemptible hypocrisy: "They threaten us with degeneracy; they cannot be educated."

It *steals* from us.

It organizes industry to cheat us. It cheats us out of our land; it cheats us out of our labor. It confiscates our savings. It reduces our wages. It raises our rent. It steals our profit. It taxes us without representation. It keeps us consistently and universally poor, and then feeds us on charity and derides our poverty.

It *insults* us.

It has organized a nation-wide and latterly a world-wide propaganda of deliberate and continuous insult and defamation of black blood wherever found. It decrees that it shall not be possible in travel nor residence, work nor play, education nor instruction for a black man to exist without tacit or open acknowledgment of his inferiority to the dirtiest white dog. And it looks upon any attempt to question or even discuss this dogma as arrogance, unwarranted assumption and treason.

108

This is the country to which we Soldiers of Democracy return. This is the fatherland for which we fought! But it is *our* fatherland. It was right for us to fight. The faults of *our* country are *our* faults. Under similar circumstances, we would fight again. But by the God of Heaven, we are cowards and jackasses if now that that war is over, we do not marshal every ounce of our brain and brawn to fight a sterner, longer, more unbending battle against the forces of hell in our own land.

We *return*.

We *return from fighting*.

We *return fighting*.

Make way for Democracy! We saved it in France, and by the Great Jehovah, we will save it in the United States of America, or know the reason why.

1919 · vol 18

LABOR OMNIA VINCIT*

Labor conquers all things — but slowly, O, so slowly. Ever the weary worldlings seek some easier, quicker way — the Way of Wealth, of Privilege, of Chance, of Power; but in the end all that they get — Food, Raiment, Palace and Pleasure — is the result of Toil, but not always of their own toil.

The great cry of world Justice today is that the fruit of toil go to the Laborer who produces it. In this labor of Production we recognize effort of all sorts — lifting, digging, carrying, measuring, thinking, foreseeing; but we are refusing to recognize Chance, Birth or Monopoly as just grounds for compelling men to serve men.

In this fight for Justice to Labor the Negro looms large. In Africa and the South Seas, in all the Americas and dimly in Asia he is a mighty worker and potentially,

* Labor conquers all

perhaps, the mightiest. But of all laborers cheated of their just wage from the world's dawn to today, he is the poorest and bloodiest.

In the United States he has taken his fastest forward step, rising from owned slave to tied serf, from servant to day laborer, from scab to half-recognized union man in less than a century. Armies, mobs, lynchers, laws and customs have opposed him, yet he lurches forward. His very so-called indolence is his dimly-conceived independence; his singing soul is his far-flaming ideal; and nothing but organized and persistent murder and violence can prevent him from becoming in time the most efficient laboring force in the modern world.

Meantime, in the world round him, the battle of Industrial Democracy is being fought and the white laborers who are fighting it are not sure whether they want their black fellow-laborer as ally or slave. If they could make him a slave, they probably would; but since he can underbid their wage, they slowly and reluctantly invite him into the union. But can they bring themselves inside the Union to regard him as a man — a fellow-voter, a brother?

No — not yet. And there lies the most stupendous labor problem of the twentieth century — transcending the problem of Labor and Capital, of Democracy, of the Equality of Women — for it is the problem of the Equality of Humanity in the world as against white domination of black and brown and yellow serfs.

1919 · vol 18

THREE HUNDRED YEARS

Three hundred years ago this month a "Dutch man of Warre sold us twenty Negars." They were not slaves. They were stolen freemen. They were free in Africa; they were free by the laws of Virginia. By force and fraud they and their children were gradually reduced to a slavery, the legality of which was not fully recognized for nearly a century after 1619. From their loins and the bodies of their fellows of after-years have sprung — counting both "white" and "black" — full twenty million souls. Those still visibly tinged with their blood are still enslaved — by compulsory ignorance, disfranchisement and public insult. In sack-cloth and ashes, then, we commemorate this day, lest we forget; lest a single drop of blood, a single moan of pain, a single bead of sweat, in all these three, long, endless centuries should drop into oblivion.

Why must we remember? Is this but a counsel of Vengeance and Hate? God forbid! We must remember because if once the world forgets evil, evil is reborn; because if the suffering of the American Negro is once forgotten, then there is no guerdon, down to the last pulse of time, that Devils will not again enslave and maim and murder and oppress the weak and unfortunate.

Behold, then, this month of mighty memories; celebrate it, Children of the Sun, in solemn song and silent march and grim thanksgiving. The Fourth Century dawns and through it, God guide our thrilling hands.

1919 · vol 18

FORWARD

We black folk easily drift into intellectual provincialism. We know our problem and tend to radical thought in its solution, but do we strive to know the problems of other forward forging groups whose difficulties are inevitably intertwined with ours?

Here, for instance, is the question of the ownership of public utilities — the railroads, the telegraph and telephone and the street cars — utilities used largely, if not primarily, by the working class, and businesses which have yielded immense fortunes to private owners in the past.

What do we think of these questions — are we studying them? Are we intelligent on the facts? Do we know that the United States is almost the only civilized country that does not own its railroads and wires, and that the municipal ownership of street transportation is widespread?

Or take the battle of North Dakota under the Non-Partisan League; are we swallowing easily the gossip of a prejudiced press, or do we realize that these western farmers are resolutely grappling with the mightiest problem of present-day life — how to prevent the necessities of the poor from being simply the opportunity of predatory wealth to amass dangerous fortunes? North Dakota is putting her government into the business of banking and publishing, running grain elevators and stockyards, packing-houses and flour mills and overseeing mines.

Will she fail? Perhaps, but her efforts are worth watching, and failure never yet proved wrong right.

Beyond these questions lie the Suffering Groups — Ireland, India, Russia.

From long tradition — since the draft riots of the Civil War — Negroes have had no sympathy with the Irish. But they must not rest in this unreason. Let every colored man read this month a history of Ireland. If he does not rise from it bitter with English cruelty and hypocrisy, he is callous indeed.

The cry of oppressed India sounds right in our own land in the persistent attempts of England to secure the transportation of Hindus accused of the treason of trying to make their country free.

And, finally, the one new Idea of the World War — the idea which may well stand in future years as the one thing that made the slaughter worth while — is an Idea which we are like to fail to know because it is today hidden under the malediction hurled at Bolshevism.

It is not the murder, the anarchy, the hate, which for

years under Czar and Revolution drenched Russia, it is the vision of great dreamers that only those who work shall vote and rule.

1919 · vol 18

THE AMERICAN LEGION

The American Legion is composed, as President Wilson tells us, of "the men who have served in the Army, Navy and Marine Corps, and who are now banding together to preserve the splendid traditions of that service."

The Legion was formed at preliminary meetings, held in Paris and St. Louis, and sought to settle the inevitable color question by giving all authority as to admitting posts to the state bodies. The South promised faithfully to treat Negroes fairly. As a result, in South Carolina "our committee was told flatly by the Executive Committee of the state organization that it was a white man's organization and that Negroes would not be admitted." In Louisiana, Negroes were also excluded; but Virginia caps the climax by offering to admit Negroes on condition that

Officers of state organization be elected by whites.

Executive Committee be elected by whites.

Time and place of meeting be fixed by whites.

Delegates to national convention to be appointed in "equitable" manner between whites and blacks by the Executive Committee.

Constitution may be amended by two-thirds vote of whites.

This action and other considerations have given impetus to several all-Negro veteran associations — The Grand Army of Americans in Washington, D. C.; The League for Democracy in New York; and The American Alliance in Richmond. There is room and work for such colored bodies, *but every Negro soldier and sailor should fight to join the American Legion*. Do not give up the battle. Organize throughout the North and South. In the North there will be little, if any, opposition. In the South every subterfuge will be sought, but force the fight. Make the bourbons refuse in writing, and then take the question to the national convention. Do not help the rascals to win by giving up.

1919 · vol 18

AGAIN, SOCIAL EQUALITY

Mr. Paleface entered his parlor mincingly — "My dear man," he said, expressively.

"I am Brownson," said the dark man quietly.

"Of course, of course — I know you well, and your people. My father was an abolitionist, and I had a black mammy —"

Mr. Brownson looked out of the window, and said rapidly:

"I have come to ask for certain rights and privileges. My people —"

"— suffer; I know it; I know it. I have often remarked what a shame it was. Sir, it is an outrage!"

"— yes; we want to ask —"

Mr. Paleface raised a deprecating finger, "Not social equality," he murmured, "I trust you are not asking that."

"Certainly not," said Brownson. "I think the right of a man to select his friends and guests and decide with whom he will commit matrimony, is sacredly his and his alone."

"Good, good! Now, my man, we can talk openly, face to face. We can pour out our souls to each other. What can I do? I have already sent my annual check to Hampton."

"Sir, we want to vote."

"Ah! That is difficult, difficult. You see, voting has

come to have a new significance. We used to confine our votes to politics, but now — bless me! — we are voting religion, work, social reform, landscape-gardening, and art. Then, too, women are in politics — you see — well, I'm sure you sense the difficulties. Moreover, what is voting? A mere form — the making and execution of the laws is the thing, and there I promise you that I —"

"Well, then; we would help in carrying out the laws."

"Commendable ambition. Very, very commendable. But this involves even greater difficulties. Administrators and executives are thrown closely together — often in the same room — at the same desk. They have to mingle and consult. Much as I deplore the fact, it is true, that a man will not sit at a desk or work at a bench with a man whose company at a theatre he would resent."

"I see," said Brownson, thoughtfully. "I presume, then, it is our business to demand this right to sit in theatres and places of popular entertainment."

"Good Lord, man, that's impossible! Civil rights like this cannot be forced. Objectionable persons must grow, develop — er wash, before —"

"Then I am sure you will help me clean and train my people. I want to join in the great movements for social uplift."

"Splendid! I will have some movements organized for your folks."

"No, I want to be part of the general movement, so as to get the training and inspiration, the wide outlook, the best plans."

"Are you crazy? Don't you know that social uplift work consists of a series of luncheons, dinners, and teas, with ladies present?"

"Um," said Brownson. "I see. I, also, see that in answering your first question, I made a mistake. In the light of your subsequent definition, I see that social equality, far from being what I don't want, is precisely what I do want."

"I knew it!" screamed Mr. Paleface. "I knew it all the time; I saw it sneaking into your eyes. You want — you dare to want to marry my sister."

"Not if she looks like you," said Brownson, "and not if she's as big a liar."

"Get out — get out — leave my house, you ungrateful —"

1919—20 · vol 19

RACE PRIDE

Our friends are hard — very hard — to please. Only yesterday they were preaching "Race Pride."

"Go to!" they said, "and be PROUD of your race."

If we hesitated or sought to explain — "Away," they yelled; "Ashamed-of-Yourself and Want-to-be-White!"

Of course, the Amazing Major is still at it, but do you notice that others say less — because they see that bull-headed worship of any "race," as such, may lead and does lead to curious complications?

For instance: Today Negroes, Indians, Chinese, and other groups, are gaining new faith in themselves; they are beginning to "like" themselves; they are discovering that the current theories and stories of "backward" peoples are largely lies and assumptions; that human genius and possibility are not limited by color, race, or blood. What is this new self-consciousness leading to? Inevitably and directly to distrust and hatred of whites; to demands for self-government, separation, driving out of foreigners: "Asia for the Asiatics," "Africa for the Africans," and "Negro officers for Negro troops!"

No sooner do whites see this unawaited development than they point out in dismay the inevitable consequences: "You lose our tutelage," "You spurn our knowledge," "You need our wealth and technique." They point out how fine is the world rôle of Elder Brother.

Very well. Some of the darker brethren are convinced. They draw near in friendship; they seek to enter schools and churches; they would mingle in industry — when lo! "Get out," yells the White World — "You're not our brothers and never will be" — "Go away, herd by yourselves" — "Eternal Segregation in the Lord!"

Can you wonder, Sirs, that we are a bit puzzled by all this and that we are asking gently, but more and more insistently, Choose one or the other horn of the dilemma:

1. Leave the black and yellow world alone. Get out of Asia, Africa, and the Isles. Give us our states and towns and sections and let us rule them undisturbed. Absolutely segregate the races and sections of the world.

Or —

2. Let the world meet as men with men. Give utter Justice to all. Extend Democracy to all and treat all men according to their individual desert. Let it be possible for whites to rise to the highest positions in China and Uganda and blacks to the highest honors in England and Texas.

Here is the choice. Which will you have, my masters?

1920 · vol 19

OF GIVING WORK

"We give you people work and if we didn't, how would you live?"

The speaker was a southern white man. He was of the genus called "good." He had come down from the Big House to advise these Negroes, in the forlorn little church which crouched on the creek. He didn't come to learn, but to teach. The result was that he did not learn, and he saw only that blank, impervious gaze which colored people know how to assume; and that dark wall of absolute silence which they have a habit of putting up instead of applause. He felt awkward, but he repeated what he had said, because he could not think of anything else to say:

"We give you people work, and if we didn't, how would you live?"

And then the old and rather ragged black man arose in the back of the church and came slowly forward and as he came, he said:

"And we gives you homes; and we gives you cotton; and we makes your land worth money; and we waits on you and gets your meals and cleans up your dirt. If we didn't do all those things for you, how would you live?"

The white man choked and got red, but the old black man went on talking:

"And what's more: we gives you a heap more than you gives us and we's getting mighty tired of the bargain —"

"I think we ought to give you fair wages," stammered the white man.

"And that ain't all," continued the old black man, "we ought to have something to say about your wages. Because if what *you* gives us gives *you* a right to say what we ought to get, then what *we* gives you gives *us* a right to say what *you* ought to get; and we're going to take that right *some day.*"

The white man blustered:

"That's Bolshevism!" he shouted.

And then church broke up.

1920 · vol 19

PAN-AFRICA

The growth of a body of public opinion among peoples of Negro descent broad enough to be called Pan-African is a movement belonging almost entirely to the twentieth century.

Seven hundred and fifty years before Christ the Negroes as rulers of Ethiopia and conquerors of Egypt were practically supreme in the civilized world; but the character of the African continent was such that this supremacy brought no continental unity; rather the inhabitants of the narrow Nile Valley set their faces toward the Mediterranean and Asia more than toward the western Sudan, the valley of the Congo and the Atlantic.

From that time even in the rise of the Sudanese kingdoms of the 13th, 14th and 15th centuries there was still no Pan-Africa; and after that the slave trade brought continental confusion.

In 1900 at the time of the Paris Exposition there was called on January 23, 24 and 25 a Pan-African Conference in Westminster Hall. London. A second conference was held at Tuskegee Institute about 1912.

Finally, at the time of the Peace Conference in Paris, February, 1919, the first Pan-African Congress was called. The interest in this congress was world-wide among the darker peoples. Delegates were elected in the United States, the West Indies, South and West Africa and elsewhere. Most of them, of course, were prevented from attending as a result of war measures and physical difficulties.

However, there did assemble in Paris, 57 delegates from 15 countries where over 85,000,000 Negroes and persons of African descent dwell. Resolutions were adopted taking up the question of the relation of Africa to the League of Nations, and the general questions of land, capital, labor, education, hygiene and the treatment of civilized Negroes. Blaise Diagne, Deputy from Senegal and Commissioner in charge of the French Colonial Troops, was elected president of a permanent organization, and W. E. B. Du Bois of the United States, Editor of *The Crisis,* was made secretary. A second congress was called to meet in Paris in September, 1921.

Meantime, the feeling of the necessity for understanding

among the Africans and their descendants has been growing throughout the world. There was held from March 11-29, 1920, the National Congress of British West Africa. This body after careful conference adopted resolutions concerning legislative reforms, the franchise, administrative changes, a West African University, commercial enterprise, judicial and sanitary programs. They also stated their opinion concerning the land question and self-determination and sent a deputation to the King. The deputation, consisting of three lawyers, two merchants, an ex-Deputy Mayor, a physician and a native ruler, went to England and presented to the King their demands, which included right to vote, local self-government, and other matters.

Other movements have gone on. In the agitation for Egyptian independence there is a large number of men of Negro descent. In South Africa, the African Political Organization and the Native Congress have had a number of conferences and have sent delegates to London, protesting against the land legislation of the Union of South Africa.

In the Canal Zone and in the West Indies have come movements looking toward union of effort among peoples of African descent and emphasizing the economic bond. In the United States there is the National Association for the Advancement of Colored People, with its 90,000 members and its very wide influence and activities.

Many of these movements will be represented in the second Pan-African Congress next fall, and out of this meeting will undoubtedly grow a larger and larger unity of thought among Negroes and through this, concerted action. At first this action will probably include a demand for political rights, for economic freedom — especially in relation to the land — for the abolition of slavery, peonage and caste, and for freer access to education. . . .

The life of Charles Young was a triumph of tragedy. No one ever knew the truth about the Hell he went through at West Point.* He seldom even mentioned it. The pain was too great. Few knew what faced him always in his army life. It was not enough for him to do well — he must always do better; and so much and so conspicuously better, as to disarm the scoundrels that ever trailed him. He lived in the army surrounded by insult and intrigue and yet he set his teeth and kept his soul serene and triumphed.

He was one of the few men I know who literally turned the other cheek with Jesus Christ. He was laughed at for it and his own people chided him bitterly, yet he persisted. When a white Southern pigmy at West Point protested at taking food from a dish passed first to Young, Young passed it to him first and afterward to himself. When officers of inferior rank refused to salute a "nigger," he saluted them. Seldom did he lose his temper, seldom complain.

With his own people he was always the genial, hearty, half-boyish friend. He kissed the girls, slapped the boys on the back, threw his arms about his friends, scattered his money in charity; only now and then behind the Veil did his nearest comrades see the hurt and pain graven on his heart; and when it appeared he promptly drowned it in his music — his beloved music, which always poured from his quick, nervous fingers, to caress and bathe his soul.

Steadily, unswervingly he did his duty. And Duty to him, as to few modern men, was spelled in capitals. It was his lode-star, his soul; and neither force nor reason swerved him from it. His second going to Africa, after a terrible attack of black water fever, was suicide. He knew it. His wife knew it. His friends knew it. He had been sent to *Africa* because the Army considered his blood

* West Point: United States Military Academy

121

pressure too high to let him go to *Europe!* They sent him there to die. They sent him there because he was one of the very best officers in the service and if he had gone to Europe he could not have been denied the stars of a General. They could not stand a black American General. Therefore they sent him to the fever coast of Africa.

They ordered him to make roads back jn the haunted jungle. He knew what they wanted and intended. He could have escaped it by accepting his retirement from active service, refusing his call to active duty and then he could have lounged and lived at leisure on his retirement pay. But Africa needed him. He did not yell and collect money and advertise great schemes and parade in crimson — he just went quietly, ignoring appeal and protest.

He is dead. But thé heart of the Great Black Race, the Ancient of Days — the Undying and Eternal — rises and salutes his shining memory: Well done! Charles Young, Soldier and Man and unswerving Friend.

1921 · vol 23

ART FOR NOTHING

There is a deep feeling among many people and particularly among colored people that Art should not be paid for. The feeling is based on an ancient and fine idea of human Freedom in the quest of Beauty and on a dream that the artist rises and should rise above paltry consideration of dollars and food.

At the same time everybody knows that artists must live if their art is to live. Everybody knows that if the people who enjoy the artist's work do not pay for it, somebody else must or his work cannot go on. Despite this practical, obvious fact, we are united with singular unity to starve colored artists.

Mrs. Meta Warrick Fuller, the sculptor, recently did a beautiful piece of work for a great social movement. She was wretchedly and inadequately paid for it; in fact, it would not be too much to say that she was not paid at all. And the movement congratulated itself upon its economy. Mrs. May Howard Jackson, whose portrait busts are a marvelous contribution to the history of the Negro, in years of work has not received a month's decent income. Mr. William A. Scott, whose painting is one of the finest things the Negro race has produced in America, has had a desperate struggle to make a living. Richard Brown died of privation while yet a boy.

Only in the case of our musicians have we been willing to pay anything like a return for their services, and even in their case we continually complain if they do not give their services for "charity." We have a few men who are trying to entertain and instruct the public through the writing of books and papers and by carefully prepared lectures. Few buy their books — they borrow them. The men are severely criticized by many because they ask pay for lectures.

All this is wrong; it is miserably wrong; it is warning away exactly the type of men who would do more than any others to establish the right of the black race to universal recognition. If work is honorable, then pay is honorable; what we should be afraid of is not overpaying the artist, but underpaying, starving and killing him.

1922 · vol 24

KICKING US OUT

From Emancipation in 1863 up until 1912 Negroes voted the Republican ticket as a matter of religion. The effort of Taft* to get rid of his obligations to the Negro vote so disgusted black men that a concerted effort was made to get Negro support for the Democrats in 1912. A special

* William Howard Taft: 27th President of the United States, 1909—13; afterwards Supreme Court judge

section of the National Democratic Campaign organization was devoted to this work and Candidate Woodrow Wilson promised the Negro "Justice, and not mere grudging Justice." He was elected, and did as near nothing to help the Negro as he possibly could. Some concessions came by sheer compulsion and war necessity but the net result was that the Democratic Party said: We do not want Negro votes.

In 1916 the Negro was between the Devil of Wilson and the Deep Sea of Taft, while Roosevelt rejected them from Bull Moose and catered to Louisiana. In 1920 Cox refused even to receive a Negro delegation and Harding* got the Negro vote. Immediately he went to Texas and Florida and consorted with the white Southern politicians. Since then it has been reported again and again that he is very desirous of building up a white Republican Party in the South; that he advises the Negro to follow white leaders and not aspire to lead himself. Finally Mr. Harding has openly and authoritatively invited at least half the Negroes to leave the Republican Party.

To some of our bewildered race this may appear not simply as a calamity but as the absolute nullification of our political power. The Democrats won't have us and the Republicans don't want us. Is there anything to do but impotently wring our empty hands?

There is. This is our opportunity; this spells our political emancipation. We are invited not to support either of the old, discredited and bankrupt political parties. In other words, we are being compelled to do what every honest thinking American wants to do — namely, support some third party which represents character, decency and ideals. Just as the two old parties have combined against us to nullify our power by a "gentleman's agreement" of non-recognition, no matter how we vote — in the same way

* Warren Gamaliel Harding: 29th President of the United States, 1921—23

they have agreed to nullify the vote of every forward-look-ing, thinking, honest American. The revolt against this smug and idiotic defiance of the demand for advanced legislation and intelligence is slowly sweeping the country.

The longer it is held back by Czaristic methods the more radical and bitter will be the eventual recoil. We are invited to join this radical reaction. We are compelled to join. We accept the invitation and rejoice in the compulsion. May God write us down as asses if ever again we are found putting our trust in either the Republican or the Democratic Parties.

1922 · vol 24

EDUCATION

There is a widespread feeling that a school is a machine. You insert a child at 9 a.m. and extract it at 4 p.m., improved and standardized with parts of Grade IV, first term. In truth, school is a desperate duel between new souls and old to pass on facts and methods and dreams from a dying world to a world in birth pains without letting either teacher or taught lose for a moment faith and interest. It is hard work. Often, most often, it is a futile failure. It is never wholly a success without the painstaking help of the parent.

Yet I know Negroes, thousands of them, who never visit the schools where their children go; who do not know the teachers or what they teach or what they are supposed to teach; who do not consult the authorities on matters of discipline — do not know who or what is in control of the schools or how much money is needed or received.

Oh, we have our excuses! The teachers do not want us around. They do not welcome co-operation. Colored parents especially may invite insult or laughter. All true in some cases. Yet the best schools and the best teachers pray for and welcome the continuous intelligent co-operation of parents. And the worst schools need it and must be made to realize their need.

There has been much recent discussion among Negroes as to the merits of mixed and segregated schools. It is said that our children are neglected in mixed schools. "Let us have our own schools. How else can we explain the host of colored High School graduates in Washington, and the few in Philadelphia?" Easily. In Washington, parents are intensely interested in their schools and have for years followed, watched and criticized them. In Philadelphia, the colored people have evinced no active interest save in *colored* schools and there is no colored High School.

Save the great principle of democracy and equal opportunity and fight segregation by wealth, class or race or color, not by yielding to it but by watching, visiting and voting in all school matters, organizing parents and children and bringing every outside aid and influence to co-operate with teachers and authorities.

In the North with mixed schools unless colored parents take intelligent, continuous and organized interest in the schools which their children attend, the children will be neglected, treated unjustly, discouraged and balked of their natural self-expression and ambition. Do not allow this. Supervise your children's schools.

In the South unless the parents know and visit the schools and keep up continuous, intelligent agitation, the teachers will be sycophants, the studies designed to make servant girls, and the funds stolen by the white trustees.

1922 · vol 24

ON BEING CRAZY

It was one o'clock and I was hungry. I walked into a restaurant, seated myself and reached for the bill-of-fare. My table companion rose.

"Sir," said he, "do you wish to force your company on those who do not want you?"

No, said I, I wish to eat.

"Are you aware, sir, that this is social equality?"

Nothing of the sort, sir, it is hunger — and I ate.

The day's work done, I sought the theatre. As I sank into my seat, the lady shrank and squirmed.

I beg pardon, I said.

"Do you enjoy being where you are not wanted?" she asked coldly.

Oh no, I said.

"Well you are not wanted here."

I was surprised. I fear you are mistaken, I said. I certainly want the music and I like to think the music wants me to listen to it.

"Usher," said the lady, "this is social equality."

No, madame, said the usher, it is the second movement of Beethoven's Fifth Symphony.

After the theatre, I sought the hotel where I had sent my baggage. The clerk scowled.

"What do you want?" he asked.

Rest, I said.

"This is a white hotel," he said.

I looked around. Such a color scheme requires a great deal of cleaning, I said, but I don't know that I object.

"We object," said he.

Then why, I began, but he interrupted.

"We don't keep niggers," he said, "we don't want social equality."

Neither do I, I replied gently, I want a bed.

I walked thoughtfully to the train. I'll take a sleeper through Texas. I'm a bit dissatisfied with this town.

"Can't sell you one."

I only want to hire it, said I, for a couple of nights.

"Can't sell you a sleeper in Texas," he maintained. "They consider that social equality."

I consider it barbarism, I said, and I think I'll walk.

Walking, I met a wayfarer who immediately walked to the other side of the road where it was muddy. I asked his reasons.

"Niggers is dirty," he said.

So is mud, said I. Moreover I added, I am not as dirty as you — at least not yet.

"But you're a nigger, ain't you?" he asked.

My grandfather was so called.

"Well then!" he answered triumphantly.

Do you live in the South? I persisted, pleasantly.

"Sure," he growled, "and starve there."

I should think you and the Negroes might get together and vote out starvation.

"We don't let them vote."

We? Why not? I said in surprise.

"Niggers is too ignorant to vote."

But, I said, I am not so ignorant as you.

"But you're a nigger."

Yes, I'm certainly what you mean by that.

"Well then!" he returned, with that curiously inconsequential note of triumph. "Moreover," he said, "I don't want my sister to marry a nigger."

I had not seen his sister, so I merely murmured, let her say, no.

"By God you shan't marry her, even if she said yes."

But — but I don't want to marry her, I answered a little perturbed at the personal turn.

"Why not!" he yelled, angrier than ever.

Because I'm already married and I rather like my wife.

"Is she a nigger?" he asked suspiciously.

Well, I said again, her grandmother — was called that.

"Well then!" he shouted in that oddly illogical way.

I gave up.

Go on, I said, either you are crazy or I am.

"We both are," he said as he trotted along in the mud.

1922 · vol 26

The Woman's Medical College of Philadelphia has recently had a most difficult and trying experience, and we are writing to commiserate with it.

You see it was this way: Dr. W. E. Atkins of Hampton, Va., colored, has a daughter, Dr. Lillian Atkins Moore. Dr. Moore is one of the best students that the Woman's Medical College ever had — which was unfortunate. Colored people ought to be fools and when they are geniuses it makes trouble.

Dr. Moore is the only colored graduate this year and was chosen secretary of the Senior Class. She won the Freshman prize in anatomy with an average of 97, passed the Medical Board with a high average and in general made herself a record most unpleasant for the authorities.

Being about to complete her course with distinction she applied October 12, 1922 for an internship in the hospital. A painful silence ensued. In fact it was not until March 2, 1923, after all internes had been appointed that Dr. Moore had this letter in answer to a reminder that her application was unanswered:

Dear Mrs. Moore; I was a little surprised to get your letter in regard to an interneship ... I had been told that we could not possibly undertake to give you a service here. We are all your good friends and it is a most unpleasant thing to have to tell you that just because you are colored we can't arrange to take you comfortably into the hospital. I am quite sure that most of the internes who come to us next year will not give us as good work as you are capable of doing; and I hope that if I can be of any service to you in helping you to secure an interneship that you will let me help.
Yours truly,
Jessie W. Pryor, M. D.
Medical Director

Meantime the woman's College made every effort to secure for Dr. Moore an internship at one of our colored hospitals. Dr. Tracy, the dean of the College, said such praiseworthy things of Dr. Moore that Dr. Turner of Douglass Hospital was constrained to ask why the College Hospital would want such an exceptional student and physician to leave them! No effort nor pressure to gain the internship availed. Still she is the best physician the College is sending out! Also she is about as white in color as Dr. Pryor herself.

There is no doubt about it, colored Americans have got to quit having brains; it's putting our white friends in all sorts of embarrassing positions.

1923 · vol 26

AFRICAN DIARY

I have just come back from a journey in the world of nearly five months. I have travelled 15,000 miles. I set foot on three continents. I have visited five countries, four African islands and five African colonies. I have sailed under five flags. I have seen a black president inaugurated. I have walked in the African big bush and heard the night cry of leopards. I have traded in African markets, talked with African chiefs and been the guest of white governors. I have seen the Alhambra and the great mosque at Cordova and lunched with H. G. Wells*; and I am full, very full with things that must be said.

December 16, 1923

Today I sailed from Tenerife for Africa. The night was done in broad black masses across the blue and the sun burned a great livid coal in the sky. Above rose the Peak

---

* Herbert George Wells (1866—1946): British author

of Tenerife, round like a woman's breast, pale with snow patches, immovable, grand.

On the boat — the *Henner* from Bremen — I am in Germany and opposite is a young man who fought four and a half years in the German army on all fronts — bitter, bitter. War is not done yet, he says. He's going to Angola.

We are six Germans in this little floating Germany: a captain, fifty or fifty-five, world roamer — San Francisco, Klondike, all Africa, *gemüthlich*, jovial; a bull-headed, red-necked first officer, stupid, good, funny; a doctor, well bred, kindly; a soldier and business man, bitter, keen, hopeful; others dumber and more uncertain. We drink Bremer beer, smoke, tell tales and the cabin rings.

December 17

On the sea — slipping lazily south, in cloud and sun and languorous air. The food is good and German. The beer is such as I have not tasted for a quarter century — golden as wine, light with almost no feel of alcohol. And I sense rather than hear a broken, beaten, but unconquered land, a spirit bruised, burned, but immortal. There is defense eager, but not apology; there is always the pointing out of the sin of all Europe.

My cabin is a dream. It is white and clean, with windows — not portholes — and pretty curtains at berth, door and window; electric light.

December 19

The languorous days are creeping lazily away. We have passed Cape Bojador of historic memory; we have passed the Tropic of Cancer, we are in the Tropics! There is a moon and by day an almost cloudless sky. I rise at eight and breakfast at eight thirty. Then I write and read until lunch at 12:30. About 1:30 I take a nap and coffee at four. Then read until 6:30 and supper. We linger at the table until nearly 9. Then reading, walking and bed by 10.

It is Thursday. Day after tomorrow I shall put my feet on the soil of Africa. As yet I have seen no land, but last night I wired to Monrovia by way of Dakar — "President King — Monrovia — Arrive Saturday, *Henner* — Du Bois."
I wonder what it all will be like? Meantime it's getting hot — *hot*, and I've put on all the summer things I've got.

December 20

Tonight the sun, a dull gold ball, strange shaped and rayless sank before a purple sky into a bright green and sinking turned the sky to violet blue and gray and the sea turned dark. But the sun itself blushed from gold to shadowed burning crimson, then to red. The sky above, blue-green; the waters blackened and then the sun did not set — it died and was not. And behind gleamed the pale silver of the moon across the pink effulgence of the clouds.

December 21

Tomorrow — Africa! Inconceivable! As yet no sight of land, but it was warm and we rigged deck chairs and lay at ease. I have been reading that old novel of mine — it has points. Twice we've wired Liberia. I'm all impatience.

December 22

Waiting for the first gleam of Africa. This morning I photographed the officers and wrote an article on Germany. Then I packed my trunk and big bag. The step for descending to the boat had been made ready. Now I read and write and the little boat runs sedately on.

3:22 p.m. — I see Africa — Cape Mount in two low, pale semicircles, so pale it looks a cloud. So my great great grandfather saw it two centuries ago. Clearer and clearer it rises and now land in a long low line runs to the right and melts into the mist and sea and Cape Mount begins.

Liberia — what a citadel for the capital of Negrodom!

When shall I forget the night I first set foot on African soil — I, the sixth generation in descent from my stolen forefathers. The moon was at the full and the waters of the Atlantic lay like a lake. All the long slow afternoon as the sun robed itself in its western scarlet with veils of misty cloud, I had seen Africa afar. Cape Mount — that mighty headland with its twin curves, northern sentinel of the vast realm of Liberia gathered itself out of the cloud at half past three and then darkened and grew clear. On beyond flowed the dark low undulating land quaint with palm and breaking sea. The world darkened. Africa faded away, the stars stood forth curiously twisted — Orion in the zenith — the Little Bear asleep and the Southern Cross rising behind the horizon. Then afar, ahead, a lone light, straight at the ship's fore. Twinkling lights appeared below, around and rising shadows.

"Monrovia," said the Captain. Suddenly we swerved to our left. The long arms of the bay enveloped us and then to the right rose the twinkling hill of Monrovia, with its crowning star. Lights flashed on the shore — here, there. Then we sensed a darker shadow in the shadows; it lay very still. "It's a boat," one said. "It's two boats." Then the shadow drifted in pieces and as the anchor roared into the deep five boats outlined themselves on the waters — great ten-oared barges black with men swung into line and glided toward us. I watched them fascinated.

Nine at Night

It was nine at night — above, the shadows, there the town, here the sweeping boats. One forged ahead with the stripes and lone star flaming behind, the ensign of the customs floating wide and bending to the long oars, the white caps of ten black sailors. Up the stairway clambered a soldier in khaki, aide-de-camp of the President of the Republic, a custom house official, the clerk of the American legation — and after them sixty-five lithe, lean black stevedores with whom the steamer would work down to Portuguese Angola and back.

A few moments of formalities, greetings and good-byes and I was in the great long boat with the President's Aide — a brown major in brown khaki. On the other side the young clerk and at the back the black, barelegged pilot. Before us on the high thwarts were the rowers: men, boys, black, thin, trained in muscle and sinew, little larger than the oars in thickness, they bent their strength to them and swung upon them.

One in the centre gave curious little cackling cries to keep the rhythm, and for the spurts, the stroke, a bit thicker and sturdier, gave a low guttural command now and then and the boat, alive, quivering, danced beneath the moon, swept a great curve to the bar to breast its narrow teeth of foam — *t'chick-a-tickity, t'chick-a-tickity* sang the boys and we glided and raced, now between boats, now near the landing — now oars aloft at the dock. And lo! I was in Africa!

December 25

Christmas eve and Africa is singing in Monrovia. They are Krus and Fanti — men, women and children and all the night they march and sing. The music was once the music of revival hymns. But it is that music now transformed and the words hidden in an unknown tongue — liquid and sonorous. It is tricked and expounded with cadence and turn. And this is that same trick I heard first in Tennessee thirty-eight years ago: The air is raised and carried by men's strong voices, while floating above in obligato, come the high mellow voices of women — it is the ancient African art of part singing so curiously and insistently different.

And so they come, gay apparelled, lit by a transparency. They enter the gate and flow over the high steps and sing and sing and sing. They saunter round the house, pick flowers, drink water and sing and sing and sing. The warm dark heat of the night steams up to meet the moon. And the night is song.

Christmas day, 1923. We walk down to the narrow, crooked wharves of Monrovia, by houses old and gray and steps like streets of stone. Before is the wide St. Paul river, double-mouthed, and beyond, the sea, white, curling on the sand. Before is the isle — the tiny isle, hut-covered and guarded by a cotton tree, where the pioneers lived in 1921. We circle round, then up the river.

Great bowing trees, festoons of flowers, golden blossoms, star-faced palms and thatched huts; tall spreading trees lifting themselves like vast umbrellas, low shrubbery with gray and laced and knotted roots — the broad, black, murmuring river. Here a tree holds wide fingers out and stretches them over the water in vast incantation; bananas throw their wide green fingers to the sun. Iron villages, scarred clearings with gray, sheet-iron homes staring grim and bare at the ancient tropical flood of green.

The river sweeps wide and the shrubs bow low. Behind, Monrovia rises in clear, calm beauty. Gone are the wharves, the low and clustered houses of the port, the tight-throated business village, and up sweep the villas and the low wall, brown and cream and white, with great mango and cotton tree, with light house and spire, with porch and pillar and the green and color of shrubbery and blossom.

We climbed the upright shore to a senator's home and received his kindly hospitality — curious blend of feudal lord and modern farmer — sandwiches, cake and champagne.

Again we glided up the drowsy river — five, ten, twenty miles and came to our hostess. A mansion of five generations with a compound of endless native servants and cows under the palm thatches. The daughters of the family wore, on the beautiful black skin of their necks, the exquisite pale gold chains of the Liberian artisan and the slim, black little granddaughter of the house had a wide pink ribbon on the thick curls of her dark hair, that lay like sudden sunlight on the shadows. Double porches, one above the other, welcomed us to ease. A native man, gay with Christmas and a dash of gin, danced and sang and danced in the road. Children ran and played in the blazing sun. We sat at a long broad table and ate duck, chicken, beef, rice, plantain and collards, cake, tea, water and Madeira wine. Then we went and looked at the heavens, the uptwisted sky — Orion and Cassiopeia at zenith; the Little Bear beneath the horizon, new unfamiliar sights in the Milky Way — all awry, a-living — sun for snow at Christmas, and happiness and cheer.

1924 · vol 27

THE CONGO

The other day, Mr. Mulligan, a young white man called upon us. He was an average American, straightforward, not college-bred but businesslike and frank. He said that he had just returned from the Belgian Congo where he had been working with the Ryan Interests! Our attention was held because much was said sometime since of the fine way in which, with Mr. Ryan as leader, United States capital was about to enter Africa and develop things. According to this young man's story, developments in the Congo Diamond Mines of Kasai are proceeding apace. In fact in some respects they went so fast that this young man could not stand them. For instance, he did not think that an unoffending native woman ought to be beaten with the rhinoceros hide whip called *chicot*. When he saw it, it sickened him so that he resigned. But the consulting engineer and others urged him not to leave but Mr. Mulligan insisted and wrote them:

When I told you that Kirk gave the woman three *chicots* over the breast, and, when I showed disapproval, then handed the *chicot* to the *capita* who slashed her at least twenty times more on all parts of her body, I do not think I exaggerated; to the contrary I think I underestimated the number. Twice or thrice during the *chicotting* the woman closed in on the *capita* and dragged the *chicot* away from him (the most pitiable scene I have ever witnessed in my life.) This only tended to infuriate Kirk more, who aided the *capita* in getting the *chicot* back, the *capita* continuing with his noble assignment. I do not care anything about the framed evidence you may now have. My story is exactly as I repeated it at the time, to which no heed was taken.

Thereupon, Mr. Mulligan wrote the following letter of resignation which was accepted by the managing engineer, and Mulligan came home:

In accordance with our conversation of yesterday I hereby resign my position with the Forminière and request to be returned home, for the following reason: I do not agree with the management's viewpoint as regards the *chicotting* of a native woman. I do not think it should be tolerated and can only consider it an American atrocity.

I regret that after eighteen months of Hell in Tshikapa I cannot stay the balance of my term, but such an incident, besides the ill feeling towards me that my expressions of sympathy for the native woman has caused, makes it necessary for my own personal reasons that I resign.

All of which goes to show that the Land of the Free and the Home of the Brave is "doing" Africa as badly as ever Belgium did.

1924 · vol 27

We all know what the Negro for the most part has meant hitherto on the American stage. He has been a lay figure whose business it was usually to be funny and sometimes pathetic. He has never, with very few exceptions, been human or credible. This, of course, cannot last. The most dramatic group of people in the history of the United States is the American Negro. It would be very easy for a great artist so to interpret the history of our country as to make the plot turn entirely upon the black man. Thus two classes of dramatic situations of tremendous import arise. The inner life of this black group and the contact of black and white.

It is going to be difficult to get at these facts for the drama and treat them sincerely and artistically because they are covered by a shell; or shall I say a series of concentric shells? In the first place comes the shell of what most people think the Negro ought to be and this makes everyone a self-appointed and preordained judge to say without further thought or inquiry whether this is untrue or that is wrong. Then secondly there comes the great problem of the future relations of groups and races not only in the United States but throughout the world.

To some people this seems to be a tremendous and imminent problem and in their wild anxiety to settle it in the only way which seems to them the right way they are determined to destroy art, religion and good common sense in an effort to make everything that is said or shown propaganda for their ideas. These two protective shells most of us recognize; but there is a third shell that we do not so often recognize, whose sudden presence fills us with astonishment; and that is the attitude of the Negro world itself.

This Negro world which is growing in self-consciousness, economic power and literary expression is tremendously sensitive. It has sore toes, nerve filled teeth, delicate eyes and quivering ears. And it has these because during its whole conscious life it has been maligned and caricatured and lied about to an extent inconceivable to those who do not know. Any mention of Negro blood or Negro life in America for a century has been occasion for an ugly picture, a dirty allusion, a nasty comment or a pessimistic forecast.

The result is that the Negro today fears any attempt of the artist to paint Negroes. He is not satisfied unless everything is perfect and proper and beautiful and joyful and hopeful. He is afraid to be painted as he is lest his human foibles and shortcomings be seized by his enemies for the purposes of the ancient and hateful propaganda.

Happy is the artist that breaks through any of these shells for his is the kingdom of eternal beauty. He will come through scarred and perhaps a little embittered, certainly astonished at the almost universal misinterpretation of his motives and aims. Eugene O'Neill* is bursting through. He has my sympathy for his soul must be lame with the enthusiasm of the blows rained upon him. But it is work that must be done. No greater mine of dramatic material ever lay ready for the great artist's hands than the situation of men of Negro blood in modern America.

1924 · vol 28

TO YOUR TENTS, O NORDICS!

Something must be done. Wills has just thoroughly beaten Madden in the prize-fight ring. Wills is black. Madden is "Nordic" — meaning Irish. Now everybody knows that a black man is inferior to a white man (except, of course, Jews, Italians and Slavs). Why then let these men contend? To prove the white man's superiority? It doesn't

* Eugene O'Neill (1888—1953): American playwright

need proof. We know it instinctively. Stop then letting white and black compete. It's wrong. If the black wins it proves nothing. If the white wins it's perfectly natural. Therefore don't let them meet. Everything possible has been done for ten years to protect the white race from Wills' fists. Dempsey has been running over the habitable globe to escape him, just as John L. Sullivan had to dodge Peter Jackson. The thing's got to stop. It's humiliating to the prestige and known ability of Englishmen, Irishmen and Germans. The best way is to keep Negroes from ever becoming prize-fighters. Starve 'em. Give 'em T. B. Do as South Carolina does in Education — brave old Palmetto State, God bless it! Just see here:

The appropriations for public education in South Carolina for 1924 were, according to the *Charleston News and Courier* as follows:

For White People: [35,000]

The University of South Carolina ...... $	476,025
The Citadel	161,143
Clemson College	91,813
Winthrop College	468,108
Medical College	120,775
Confederate Home College	5,000
Howe School	48,206
School for Deaf and Blind	125,700
Training School for Feeble Minded	150,310
Industrial School for Boys	129,548
Industrial School for Girls	27,170
	$1,803,798

For Colored People: [32,000]

Colored College .... $	101,150
Reformatory for Negro Boys	52,287
	$ 153,437

One of the best methods of getting rid of smart Negro competitors is to "forget." This is the brilliant invention of Dean Ignatius M. Wilkinson of Fordham University and was first used in the case of Mrs. Whaley who went and won prizes. But it availed her little — the dean forgot to print her name! and withheld her diploma for complaining!

And then — we blush to mention it — that brilliant North Carolinian who objected to a Negro in the Columbia dormitories flunked his examinations; my God! what is Columbia thinking of!

We'll bet a cooky that "intelligence" tests applied in Charleston would prove black men fools forever. That's the way to do it. Get 'em while they're young and there'll be no Harry Wills to black the beautiful blue eyes of Mr. Madden and no danger of black brains ever arguing successfully with whites. To your tents, O Nordics!

1924 · vol 28

INTERMARRIAGE

The Ku Klux Klan has secured the introduction of bills into certain legislatures, including Ohio, Iowa and Michigan, which should be called proposals *to encourage prostitution and degrade women of Negro descent.* These bills have secured the backing of Christian ministers, women's clubs and some prominent citizens, because they prevent legal marriage between persons of different races.

It is astonishing that muddled thinking will lead to such indefensible and disgraceful proposals. There is nothing to prevent today a white man from refusing to marry a colored woman. There is no law compelling a white woman to take a Negro mate. Decent custom in all civilized communities compels the scoundrel who seduces a girl to marry her no matter what race she belongs to. Does decency ask change in such custom? There are laws which say that if white people wish to consort with colored people they must marry. Can civilization demand less?

Must Nordic culture admit that the only way to prevent intermarriage is to make it illegal and if they admit this can they prove it? Mississippi makes inter-racial marriage illegal and Mississippi has 122,000 acknowledged mulattoes. The whole South refuses to black girls any adequate protection against white brutes or gentlemen and yet the South admits to a million and half mulattoes.

If reason and science, social pressure and parental advice cannot keep white and colored folk from intermarriage, will law do it? Shame on a race and a people that must stoop to such measures in order to maintain their vaunted superiority.

1925 · vol 29

LOUISVILLE, KENTUCKY

Have you noticed, brethren, that since the afflatus of post-war "science" and the great and *ex-cathedra* utterances of those mighty scientists, McDougall of Harvard and what-you-may-call-him of Princeton — that since all this flare up and proof of Negro "inferiority" by "intelligence" tests, there has dropped a significant silence? Truly the high schools and Chautauquas, the magazines and city editors are still presenting the triumphant results of the "Alpha" tests during the draft; but real scientists are going a bit slow. Why?

Well, here is one of the reasons: In Louisville, Kentucky, they have been testing school children. They had in expert psychologists and turned them loose on the children, white and black. And then? Well and then, silence; Silence!

A little bird whispered to the editor and he wrote a polite note to the Superintendent of Louisville City Schools asking for the published results of the "Intelligence" tests. Silence.

A number of the local colored school teachers asked.

Silence. The editor wrote again and even more politely, enclosing a stamp, and the reply came:

> *I have your letter of July 17. We are constantly making tests in the Louisville schools but this information is not available to the public.*
>> *Very truly yours,*
>>> *(Signed) B. W. Hartley*
>>> *Superintendent*

What is wrong? Why all this heavy secrecy? Tell it not in Gath, but if the truth must be known, those damned tests went and came out wrong! In other words, instead of proving white children superior they actually proved — but no; we cannot write it; it's too awful.

But what difference does it make anyhow? Who needs psychology or evolution or anthropology or anything else to prove Nordic superiority? Doesn't everybody know it without proof . . . ?

Meantime to Louisville in its misery we make the suggestion: Don't publish all the results, publish the parts you like best. Or better, wait and publish only those which come out right!

1925 · vol 30

THE CHALLENGE OF DETROIT

In Detroit, Michigan, a black man has shot into a mob which was threatening him, his family, his friends and his home in order to make him move out of the neighborhood. He killed one man and wounded another.

Immediately a red and awful challenge confronts the nation. Must black folk shoot and shoot to kill in order to maintain their rights or is this unnecessary and wanton bloodshed for fancied ill? The answer depends on the facts. The Mayor of Detroit has publicly warned both mob and Negroes. He has repudiated mob law but he adds, turning to his darker audience, that they ought not to invite aggression by going where they are not wanted. There are thus two interpretations:

1. A prosperous Negro physician of Detroit, seeking to get away from his people, moves into a white residential section where his presence for social reasons is distasteful to his neighbors.

2. A prosperous Negro physician of Detroit, seeking a better home with more light, air, space and quiet, finds it naturally in the parts of the city where white folk with similar wants have gone rather than in the slums where most of the colored are crowded.

Which version is true? See the figures:

Negro Population of Detroit
1900 . .   4,111
1910 . .   5,741
1920 . . 40,838
1925 . . 60,000 (estimated)

Two thirds of this population in 1920 were crowded into three wards — the Third, Fifth and Seventh. Meantime the total population of Detroit has more than doubled in ten years and the people have reached out on all sides to new dwelling places. Have the Negroes no right to rush too? Is it not their duty to seek better homes and, if they do, are they not bound to "move into white neighborhoods" which is simply another way of saying "move out of congested slums?"

Why do they not make their own new settlements then? Because no individual can make a modern real estate development; no group of ordinary individuals can compete with organized real estate interests and get a decent deal. When Negroes have tried it they have usually had miserable results; in Birmingham, Alabama, twenty years since, they bought a nice street and lined it with pretty homes; the city took all its prostitutes and stuck them into a segregated vice district right behind the pretty homes! In Macon, Savannah, New Orleans and Atlanta crime and prostitution have been kept and protected in Negro residence districts. In New York City, for years, no Negro could rent or buy a home in Manhattan outside the "Tenderloin"; and white Religion and Respectability far from stretching a helping hand turned and cursed the blacks when by bribery, politics and brute force they broke into the light and air of Harlem. Some great leaders in Negro philanthropy like Clarence Kelsey formed a financial bloc to push the Negroes out of Harlem, to refuse mortgages to landlords renting to them; but only one practical project of furnishing them decent quarters came to fruition.

Dear God! Must we not live? And if we live may we not live somewhere? And when a whole city full of white folk led and helped by banks, Chambers of Commerce, mortgage companies and "realtors" are combing the earth for every decent bit of residential property for whites, where in the name of God can we live and live decently if not by these same whites? If some of the horror-struck and law-worshipping white leaders of Detroit instead of winking at the Ku Klux Klan and admonishing the Negroes to allow themselves to be kicked and killed with impunity — if these would finance and administer a decent scheme of housing relief for Negroes it would not be necessary for us to kill white mob leaders in order to live in peace and decency. These whited sepulchres pulled that trigger and not the man that held the gun.

But, wail the idiots, Negroes depress real estate values! This is a lie — an ancient and bearded lie. Race prejudice decreases values both real estate and human; crime, ignorance and filth decrease values. But a decent, quiet, educated family buying property in a decent neighborhood will not affect values a bit unless the people in that neighborhood hate a colored skin more than they regard the value of their own property. This has been proven in a thousand instances. Sudden fall in values comes through propaganda and hysteria manipulated by real estate agents or by Southern slave drivers who want their labor to return South; or by ignorant gossip mongers. Usually Negroes do not move into new developments but into districts which well-to-do whites are deserting. The fall in values is not due to race but to a series of economic readjustments and often, as in Baltimore, real estate values were actually saved and raised, not lowered, when black folk bought Druid Hill Avenue and adjacent streets. Certainly a flood of noisy dirty black folk will ruin any neighborhood but they ruin black property as well as white, and the reason is not their color but their condition. And whom, High Heaven, shall we blame for that?

But these facts make no difference to organized American Negro haters. They are using every effort to maintain and increase race friction. In the South time and time again communities have almost forgotten race lines until the bitter, hate-preaching liar stirred it up again. The whole present "Anglo-Saxon" and "race purity" agitation in Virginia has arisen because one white family openly acknowledged its colored grandmother!

The whole crusade in Detroit has come to a head because, in 1920, 663,000 Southern whites had migrated and were living in Wisconsin, Michigan, Illinois, Indiana and Ohio. Their numbers are swelling. They are largely clerks, artisans and laborers, not illiterate but ignorant of the modern world and forming by habit the lawless material of mobs. They are ruining the finer democracy of the Middle West and using the Negro as an excuse.

What shall we do? I know a black man. He is a professional man and a graduate of a great eastern school. He has studied abroad. His wife was educated in a good western school and is a quiet housewife. His son is a college graduate and a high school teacher. They have never been arrested. They conduct themselves as cultured folk. This man is living in an apartment in Harlem. He would like more air and sunlight and less noise. He would like a new, small, modern house in the further Bronx or in the hills of Westchester or New Jersey or in the higher part of Queens. He sees daily in the papers new homes advertised suitable to his means — $500, $1,000 even $2,000 down, the rest as rent. Can he buy one of these? Not without plotting, deception, insult or murder.

For instance: A man bought a modest home in Staten Island. He was a mail carrier with a fine record; his wife was a school teacher, educated and well-bred. They had four sturdy children in school. As a result he has been mobbed and insulted, his property injured, his glass and shrubbery broken, his insurance cancelled, his life threatened, his existence made miserable. His neighbors do everything to insult him and his, even to crossing the street to avoid passing him. He sticks to his home even though offered a profit to sell, "on principle." He is "colored."

Another man in Detroit bought a fine home in a former exclusive district which is now changing. He was a physician with a large practice, the founder of a hospital, public-spirited and well-liked. He had married the daughter of perhaps the greatest of the interpreters of Negro folk songs with world-wide reputation. He moved in. A mob of thousands appeared, yelling and cursing. They broke his windows, threw out his furniture and he and his family escaped under police protection. He gave up his home, made no resistance, moved back whence he came, filed no protest, made no public complaint. He was "colored."

A little later another physician in Detroit bought another beautiful home and moved in. A mob — almost the same mob — came, cursed, threw stones and ordered him to move. He gathered his family and friends within and locked the door. Five or six thousand people lined the streets. The police set traffic officers to divert the traffic that could not get through. The mob invaded his yard and approached his doors. He shot and shot to kill. His wife and his friends are now in jail charged with *Murder in the first degree!* He was "colored."

Gentle Reader, which of these three examples shall my friend of Harlem follow? Which would you follow if you were "free," black and twenty-one?

1925 · vol 31

PHILIPPINE MULATTOES

You will have noticed in the press a delicately worded appeal for funds. It would seem that there are some little children in need in the Philippines. Major General Wood, Governor of the Islands, is speaking in their behalf:

> Chief Justice William Howard Taft of the Supreme Court of the United States, former Governor General of the Philippines, W. Cameron Forbes, Major Gen. James G. Harbord, Major Gen. Hugh L. Scott, Martin Egan, Vice-President Charles G. Dawes and dignitaries of the Catholic and Protestant churches are typical of the men who have pledged their support to this drive for funds. General Wood has cabled:

> *The American people have been so generous in their responses to the cries of children all over the world that I have no hesitation in appealing to them for children of their own blood who are in need of help. Especially do I have profound confidence, as the problem involves the honor of the American nation.*

What is all this about? In plain, cold English, the American people in bringing Peace and Civilization to the Philippines have left 18,000 bastards in the islands! Isn't this fine work? Can you not see the Godly White Race struggling under the Black Man's Burden! Can you not see how Americans hate Social Equality with brown women?

Why is America asked to support these illegitimate victims of white men's lust? Because the United States government, the War Department and Governors Wood, Taft and Forbes have somehow let American skunks scuttle from the island and leave their helpless and innocent bastards to beg and perish, and their deserted mothers to starve or serve as prostitutes to white newcomers.

Send, in God's name, America, two million dollars to Mary Frances Kern at 8 West Fortieth Street, New York, now; and send simultaneously two million protests to Washington to lambaste the heads of Congressmen who permit the holding of the Philippines as a house of prostitution for American white men under the glorious stars and stripes.

1925 · vol 31

RUSSIA, 1926

I am writing this in Russia. I am sitting in Revolution Square opposite the Second House of the Moscow Soviets and in a hotel run by the Soviet Government. Yonder the sun pours into my window over the domes and eagles and pointed towers of the Kremlin. Here is the old Chinese wall of the inner city; there is the gilded glory of the Cathedral of Christ, the Savior. Thro' yonder gate on the vast Red Square, Lenin sleeps his last sleep, with long lines of people peering each day into his dead and speaking face. Around me roars a city of two millions — Holy Moscow.

I have been in Russia something less than two months.

I did not see the Russia of war and blood and rapine. I know nothing of political prisoners, secret police and underground propaganda. My knowledge of the Russian language is sketchy and of this vast land, the largest single country on earth, I have traveled over only a small, a very small part.

But I have had certain advantages; I have seen something of Russia. I have traveled over two thousand miles and visited four of its largest cities, many of its towns, the Neva, Dnieper, Moscow and Volga of its rivers, and stretches of land and village. I have looked into the faces of its races — Jews, Tartars, Gypsies, Caucasians, Armenians and Chinese. To help my lack of language I have had personal friends, whom I knew before I came to Russia, as interpreters. They were born in Russia and speak English, French and German. This, with my English, German and French, has helped the language difficulty, but did not, of course, solve it.

I have not done my sight seeing and investigation in gangs and crowds nor according to the program of the official Foreign Bureau; but have in nearly all cases gone alone with one Russian speaking friend. In this way I have seen schools, universities, factories, stores, printing establishments, government offices, palaces, museums, summer colonies of children, libraries, churches, monasteries, boyar houses, theatres, moving-picture houses, day nurseries and co-operatives. I have seen some celebrations — self-governing children in a school house of an evening and 200,000 children and youths marching on Youth Day. I have talked with peasants and laborers, Commissars of the Republic, teachers and children.

Alone and unaccompanied I have walked the miles of streets in Leningrad, Moscow, Nijni Novgorod and Kiev at morning, noon and night; I have trafficked on the curb and in the stores; I have watched crowds and audiences and groups. I have gathered some documents and figures, plied officials and teachers with questions and sat still and gazed at this Russia, that the spirit of its life and people might enter my veins.

I stand in astonishment and wonder at the revelation of Russia that has come to me. I may be partially deceived and half-informed. But if what I have seen with my eyes and heard with my ears in Russia is Bolshevism, I am a Bolshevik.

1926 · vol 33

LYNCHINGS

The recent horrible lynchings in the United States, even the almost incredible burning of human beings alive, have raised not a ripple of interest, not a single protest from the United States Government, scarcely a word from the pulpit and not a syllable of horror or suggestion from the Defenders of the Republic, the 100 % Americans, or the propagandists of the army and navy. And this in spite of the fact that the cause of the Louisville, Mississippi, bestiality was, according to the Memphis *Commercial-Appeal*, "widespread indignation at the refusal of the Negroes traveling in slow, second-handed Fords to give road to faster cars." And yet hiding and concealing this barbarism by every resource of American silence, we are sitting in council at Geneva and Peking and trying to make the world believe that we are a civilized nation.

1927 · vol 34

BOLSHEVISM

The *Herald-Tribune* of New York thinks that it is good politics to find every now and then Bolshevism rampant among American Negroes. Nonsense! If we were a few years further from slavery than we are the Republican campaign managers would not need to invent bogeys; and we suggest the following reasons:

First, the burning of people alive in oil down in Mississippi without a single word of protest from the Gentleman who is capering around the Black Hills.

Secondly the fact that the University Travel Association of 285 Madison Avenue, New York, which is taking shiploads of students to study the modern world, writes to a young colored man of Kansas: "We are sorry but colored students are not eligible." While, on the other hand, the Student Council of New York, working in connection with the Russian Student Bureau, not only invites but urges Negro students to visit Russia; and some have gone.

1927 · vol 34

STUPIDITY

Americans are remarkably stupid. They have just completed in Indianapolis a separate high school for Negro students; the first that the city has ever had. And yet the President of the National Education Association at Seattle says that the American school system is the "greatest kindergarten of Democracy ever conceived!"

In the face of such contradictions we blunder ahead. We import millions of slaves and complain because there are Negroes in the United States. We mix black and white blood and shriek for racial purity. We open the doors to foreign immigrants and inveigh against the foreign born. We establish public schools in this democracy and then force the Catholics into separate schools by deliberately misreading all Catholic history; force Italians into Parochial schools by giving them poor accommodations and worse teachers in the public schools; and finally force a whole system of separate public schools upon Negroes because they are socially too weak to resist.

Finally, we work every device to keep Jews, Negroes and foreigners out of the most aristocratic of our colleges. Then, with long faces, we remark that Democracy is a failure. Americans are remarkably stupid.

1927 · vol 34

TEN YEARS

It is astonishing to see the determination with which those who believe in the industrial methods of America and Western Europe are spreading misinformation concerning the Russian experiment. The central thing which has happened in Russia is this: the rotten, horrible, inexpressibly brutal and silly tyranny of the Czar, has been definitely and finally overthrown. No such travesty on decent government has existed elsewhere in Europe in modern days. It was a stench in the nostrils of humanity. It was flamboyant and impudent with murder and cruelty, on a foundation of ignorance and poverty and with flaming towers of ostentation and show which completely captivated the organized snobbery of the world. To be presented at the Russian Imperial Court was the last round in the ladder of ambition for every social climber in Europe and America.

The rottenness of the Czar's Government was repeatedly exposed to the liberal world. Not a finger was raised to help. On the contrary, when in desperation Russia rose in 1905 to shake off medieval despotism and establish modern democracy, Western Europe poured its treasure into the hands of the Czar to beat the wretched Revolutionists back. Now finally, when of their own strength and determination, and their own vast will to sacrifice, the Russian people have buried Czarism and tried to establish a new government that frankly faces the economic problem which the world fears to face, there is scarcely a news-paper in America that will give this experiment even decent hearing. Yet the Union of Socialist Soviet Republics is celebrating today its Tenth Anniversary, and here's hoping that this is but the first decade toward its hundred years.

1927 · vol 34

BLEEDING IRELAND

No people can more exactly interpret the inmost meaning of the present situation in Ireland than the American Negro. The scheme is simple. You knock a man down and then have him arrested for assault. You kill a man and then hang the corpse for murder. We black folk are only too familiar with this procedure. In a given city, a mob attacks us unprepared, unsuspecting, and kills innocent and harmless black workingmen in cold blood. The bewildered Negroes rush together and begin to defend themselves. Immediately by swift legerdemain the mob becomes the militia or a gang of "deputy sheriffs." They search, harry and kill the Negroes. They disarm them and loot their homes, and when the city awakes after the "race riot," the jail is filled with Negroes charged with rioting and fomenting crime!

So in Ireland! The Irish resist, as they have resisted for hundreds of years, various and exasperating forms of English oppression. Their resistance is called crime and under ordinary conditions would be crime; in retaliation not only the "guilty" but the innocent among them are murdered and robbed and public property is burned by English guardians of the Peace!

All this must bring mingled feelings of dismay to Irishmen. No people in the world have in the past gone with blither spirit to "kill niggers" from Kingston to Delhi and from Kumassi to Fiji. In the United States,

Irish influence not only stood behind the mob in Cincinnati, Philadelphia and New York, but still stands in the American Federation of Labor to keep out Negro workingmen.

All this contains no word of argument against the ultimate freedom of Ireland — which God speedily grant! — but it does make us remember how in this world it is the Oppressed who have continually been used to cow and kill the Oppressed in the interest of the Universal Oppressor.

1928—29 · vol 34

THE HOUSE OF THE BLACK BURGHARDTS

If one slips out the northern neck of Manhattan and flies to the left of the silver Sound, one swoops in time onto the Golden River; and dodging its shining beauty, now right, now left, one comes after a hundred miles of lake, hill and mountain, in the Old Bay State. Then at the foot of high Mt. Everett one takes a solemn decision: left is sweet, old Sheffield; but pass it stolidly by and slip gently right into tiny South Egremont which always sleeps. Then wheel right again and come to Egremont Plain and the House of the Black Burghardts.

It is the first home that I remember. There my mother was born and all her nine brothers and sisters. There perhaps my grandfather was born, although that I do not know. At any rate, on this wide and lovely plain, beneath the benediction of gray-blue mountain and the low music of rivers, lived for a hundred years the black Burghardt clan. Up and to the east on a hill of rocks was Uncle Ira; down and to the south was Uncle Harlow in a low, long, red house beside a pond — in a house of secret passages, sudden steps, low, narrow doors and unbelievable furniture. And here right in the center of the world was Uncle 'Tallow, as Grandfather Othello was called.

155

It was a delectable place—simple, square and low, with the great room of the fireplace, the flagged kitchen, half a step below, and the lower woodshed beyond. Steep, strong stairs led up to Sleep, while without was a brook, a well and a mighty elm. Almost was I born there myself but that Alfred Du Bois and Mary Burghardt honeymooned a year in town and then brought me as a baby back to Egremont Plain.

I left the home as a child to live in town again and go to school. But for furtive glimpses I did not see the house again for more than a quarter century. Then riding near on a chance journey I suddenly was homesick for that house. I came to the spot. There it stood, old, lonesome, empty. Its windowless eyes stared blindly on the broad, black highway to New York. It seemed to have shrunken timidly into itself. It had lost color and fence and grass and up to the left and down to the right its sister homes were gone—dead and gone with no stick nor stone to mark their burial.

From that day to this I desperately wanted to own that house for no earthly reason that sounded a bit like sense. It was 130 long miles from my work. It was decrepit almost beyond repair save that into its tough and sturdy timbers the black Burghardts had built so much of their own dumb pluck that—

"Why the stairs don't even creak!" said She, climbing gingerly aloft.

But I fought the temptation away. Yachts and country estates and limousines are not adapted to my income. Oh, I inquired of course. The replies were discouraging. And once every year or so I drove by and stared sadly; and even more sadly and brokenly the House of the Black Burghardts stared back.

Then of a sudden Somebody whose many names and places I do not know sent secret emissaries to me on a birthday which I had firmly resolved *not* to celebrate. Sent emissaries who showed me all the Kingdoms of this

World. including something in green with a cupola; and also The House; and I smiled at the House. And they said by telegram: *The House of the Black Burghardts is come home again — it is yours!*

Whereat in great joy I celebrated another birthday and drew plans. And from its long hiding-place I brought out an old black pair of tongs. Once my grandfather, and mayhap his, used them in the great fireplace of the House. Long years I have carried them tenderly over all the earth. The sister shovel, worn in holes, was lost. But when the old fireplace rises again from the dead on Egremont Plain, its dead eyes shall see not only the ghosts of old Tom and his son Jack and his grandson Othello and his great grandson, me — but also the real presence of these iron tongs resting again in fire worship in the House of the Black Burghardts.

1928 · vol 35

PURITANS AND QUAKERS

In these days of hectic news gathering, one makes speeches and then explains them. Recently, I have been talking about Puritans in Boston and Quakers in Philadelphia. If my audience had been foreign or Western, I should have stressed the well-known and indispensable help which Puritans and Quakers have given the American Negroes for centuries. But speaking to those who knew all this and who were in danger of ancestor worship and of historical misstatement, I sought to emphasize the fact that both Puritans and Quakers enslaved Negroes. I remind my hearers that we are prone to conceive that the good of the world is done by persons not human as we are and that the ancestors of certain groups were effective because they were without sin and narrowness.

I reminded my colored audience in Boston that if the ancestors of most Americans should appear, we would all be quite ashamed of them; that as a matter of fact, the Puritans had no stainless record in their relations to Negroes. They established one of the first slave codes in America; they made fortunes in the slave trade; and if their land had been adapted to the Plantation System, they probably would have emulated Virginia.

But, I maintained, this is the hopeful side of human progress. America was settled by prostitutes and jailbirds, as well as by Puritans, Cavaliers and Negroes. And out of this heterogeneous mass had come this vast and great country. It was significant that this Tercentenary of the landing of the Pilgrims was being celebrated today not simply by their lineal descendants but by Irishmen, Italians and Negroes, all of whom Puritans had at various times persecuted.

In the case of Quakers, I pointed out that the protest against the slave trade in 1688 was made by German immigrants and not by English Friends; and that it was eight years before the Quakers advised any limitations on the buying of slaves; sixty-six years before they made the slave trade a matter of discipline; and eighty-eight years before they made manumission compulsory.

All this is not a criticism, so much as looking our enthusiasms straight in the face and being able, with all our thankfulness and appreciation, to see faults and hurts. We know perfectly well that even today life for the Negro in Puritan New England and in Quaker Pennsylvania is no bed of roses. There is much discrimination and prejudice. But hope lies in the fact that out of worse race hatred in the past, we have by our own efforts and the help of good men who continually rise here and there, come as far as we have.

This was my thesis. It was curiously misinterpreted in many ways. The Cleveland *Plaindealer* learns editorially that I said that the Puritans were prostitutes and jailbirds! While many Quakers are hurt by a criticism which seems to ignore their long and well-known efforts in behalf of the Negro. Of course, the *Plaindealer* is mistaken and the Quakers misjudge me. I am not trying to decry or forget good work. I am seeking to set the facts straight.

1930 · vol 37

ECONOMIC DISFRANCHISEMENT

There is no universal suffrage in modern industry. So far as the government conducts industry, as in the case of the post office and, in some instances, the transportation system, universal political suffrage indirectly controls the industry. But there are great public services, like the railroad, the telephone, gas and electric lighting, the telegraph and others, where the industry, although public in nature, is private in ownership, and conducted by an autocracy, except insofar as public opinion and the granting of privileges and franchises give remote control to the voters.

The disfranchisement, therefore, of the mass of workers in this case is the most extraordinary and vital disfranchisement in the modern world. When we talk of industrial democracy, we mean the increased right of the working people to determine the policies of great public services, either through direct public ownership or by private negotiation in the shape of shop committees, working agreements and the like.

What is the attitude of the Negro here? Most Negroes would have no attitude at all, so far as public ownership was concerned. They would not be interested; and yet, they are, or should be, tremendously interested. Take, for instance, the telephone service. It is well-nigh universal. The number of telephones in use by colored people runs into the millions. It is not possible that Negroes in the United States spend less than $10,000,000 a year for telephone service, and they may spend three times as much as this. In the organization of work and trade a balance is always assumed between a service rendered or goods delivered on one side and a reciprocal service rendered and goods delivered, on the other. If the exchange is not direct, it must be indirect, or the whole industrial combination fails. Yet in the case of the colored people and the telephone, there is no reciprocity. The Telephone Company in the North, almost without exception, employs no colored help whatsoever; no laborers, no telephone girls, no clerks, no officials. The whole service is absolutely closed to Negroes. In the South, a few colored men are employed as laborers and linemen, but not many.

Here then is a situation where a quasi-public institution absolutely refuses to let millions of citizens earn a decent living, while taxing them along with other citizens for this public service. This compulsory exclusion is, of course, not confined to colored people. It is exercised against Jews; it is exercised against various groups of foreign-born; it is exercised even against certain social classes among American-born citizens. But in the case of the Negroes, we can see it openly, just as in those chemical experiments where an artificially colored liquid reveals diffusion and reaction.

What now must Negroes do? If this sort of thing goes on, then disfranchisement in industry is going to be a vital factor in their elimination from modern civilization. By consolidations and mergers, by holding companies and interlocking directorates, the great industries of the world are becoming integrated into vast private organizations, which means that the work of the world — the skilled work, the best paid work — in the vast majority of the cases, is subject to this social and racial exclusion; to this refusal to allow certain classes of men to earn a decent living.

It is an intolerable situation. Attempts have been made to correct it by appeal. In Chicago and in High Harlem, New York, these appeals have been effective in the case of small store chains, and even to a slight extent with a corporation like the Western Union Telegraph Company.

But the Telephone Company remains adamant. The Gas Company is absolutely deaf and unsympathetic.

In this case there is only one thing to do, and that is for the Negro voters, with intelligence and far-reaching memory, to see that by their votes no further privileges and franchises are granted to these public service companies; and to see that the work of these companies, just as far as possible and as soon as possible, is transferred to the government. Government ownership is the only solution for this present industrial disfranchisement of the Negro.

1930 · vol 37

PATIENT ASSES

I met my friend one morning on Seventh Avenue as we were hurrying opposite ways to our work. She asked:

"Did you attend the Smuts lecture?"

I did not.

She said: "He does not strike me as sincere."

I quite agreed with her.

And then she said: "You were wise in advocating Pan-Africanism."

I thanked her. I was glad that she saw the point. I wished again, as I have often wished, that other people would see it. Here was a statesman from the Union of South Africa. Effort was made before his visit to the United States to commit the colored people to support of him and his policy in order that their action might influence their colored brethren in South Africa. As he was about to arrive, a movement was put on foot to get colored leaders to sign a laudatory address and thank Jan Smuts for his South African Negro program! This was fortunately blocked. Then a quiet conference was arranged in Washington by the Phelps Stokes Fund in which the program was confined to carefully restricted discussion of the American race problem and arranged so as to include no single Negro who had been in South Africa or had expert knowledge of the South African situation.

Meanwhile, however, Mr. Smuts, himself, supplied a good deal of missing information. He had no sooner opened his mouth at Town Hall, New York City, than he put his own foot deeply and completely in it. He compared Negroes to patient asses and wanted them to dance and sing! Negroes have been more patient than most asses and asses do not usually dance and sing. Indeed, the animals that dance and sing best are the least patient with demagogs like Smuts.

Dr. Moton of Tuskegee, who among a half-dozen Negro leaders sat upon the platform, was the only one who had the courage to challenge Smuts then and there. We congratulate him upon the deed.

Smuts explained. He meant nothing derogative. He was complimenting Negroes. That is Smuts all over! Shrewd, wary, insincere, distrusted throughout South Africa by black and white, Boer and Briton, desperately trying to pose in Europe and America as a great Liberal and forever damned by his determination to keep black folk in eternal subjection to white, while salving the fools with fair words, Hertzog, his opponent and the present Premier, is at least sincere. He is as narrow in his "nigger" hatred as Smuts, but his narrowness is lack of knowledge and not deliberate and suave hypocrisy. Hertzog wants to learn. Smuts will never learn. He knows it all now.

He ought to know it. He and his party established the color caste of South Africa in its present form. From the founding of the Union of South Africa until 1924, Smuts has been a member of the Cabinet and often Prime Minister. During this time he helped establish and vigorously defended the following caste system for black men:

1. Disfranchisement of all persons of Negro descent, except in Cape Colony, and even there Negro voters can not vote for Negro candidates.
2. Disarming the natives by excluding them from the militia.
3. Depriving natives of their land and prohibiting them from buying land except in restricted areas. This legislation gave a million and a half whites 87 percent of the land and five million natives 13 percent.
4. Excluding Negroes from the Civil Service.
5. Jim Crow regulations for railroads and public buildings. There are separate Post Offices for blacks, either at the back of the white Post Office or underground. Even here, no native clerk is employed and natives must take off their hats when entering any public building. Often they cannot walk on the sidewalk.
6. Direct taxation on natives, at the rate of $5 to $10 a year and using most of this money for the benefit of the whites, who pay no poll tax.
7. Educational facilities are so meagre that 95 percent of the natives are illiterate. In the Transvaal for a long time the government grant to native schools was about the same sum as they expended for the upkeep of animals in the Pretoria Zoo.
8. The pass system which compels every native to be registered and carry a pass without which he is subject to arrest and imprisonment.

Some of these regulations do not apply to persons of mixed blood and educated natives not living in tribes, but even for them the caste discrimination and restrictions are humiliating and disgraceful and make South Africa the worst place on earth for colored folk to live.

Conceive what would happen to an Englishman who had treated Irishmen in this way and who came to the United States to lecture? How many Irishmen would be sitting on his platform grinning at him? We certainly are patient asses. We shall never secure emancipation from the tyranny of the white oppressor until we have achieved it in our own souls.

VIRGINIA

It is with difficulty that one keeps from laughing over the plight of Virginia and its "race purity" legislation. For something like 311 years, whites, Negroes and Indians have been intermarrying and intermingling in this state. Recently, the Legislature has been trying to unscramble the races, and some papers, like the *Times-Dispatch*, are getting quite hysterical about it. Essex County, for instance, has a number of "colored" children in the white schools — that is, children in whom experts may seem to see blood that is not pure "white." "Mixed schools!" yells the *Times-Dispatch* in its frantic desire to keep these poor babies out of the best schools of the community. But some of the Indians object. It is a little hard to distinguish between Negro and Indian blood, and these folks want the benefit of the doubt. But the *Times-Dispatch* gnashes its teeth and orders the Legislature to pass a law defining a colored person as one having "any ascertainable amount of Negro blood." But this surely is not enough. Does the *Times-Dispatch* want its sister to marry a man who has an unascertainable amount of Negro blood? My God! What a loophole!

ROTTEN BOROUGHS

G. D. Williamson of Decatur, Alabama, writing in the *New York Times* of August 21 concerning the prospects of Senator Heflin's reelection, said:

"Alabama has fewer than 250,000 total voting strength."

With this total voting strength of 250,000, Alabama has been sending 10 representatives to Congress, while the State of New York, with a voting strength (election of 1928) of 4,400,000, has been allowed only 43 representatives instead of 176. In other words, every Alabama voter has apparently four and a half times the political strength of a voter in New York.

One would like to ask Mr. Williamson just how this happens? With the figures at command, *The Crisis* is unable to explain it. We find, for instance, that in 1920, according to the Census, there were 1,143,395 persons, 21 years of age and over in Alabama. And yet, only 250,000 of these vote.

Nor does the race problem wholly explain this matter, since only 441,130 of these potential voters were of Negro descent. Let us assume that all of these black folk, educated and illiterate, wealthy and paupers, were disfranchised out of hand. There would still be in Alabama 702,265 white persons who were possible voters.

There is, of course, the possibility that in Alabama it is not ladylike for a woman to vote. Whether this is the decision of the women or the men, we are not certain. But suppose we subtract from these possible white voters all of the Alabama women twenty-one and more years, who amounted in 1920 to 344,209. There are still left 358,056 male white citizens of Alabama who presumably should vote on the basis of the population of 1920. Since then, the population has increased by 263,826 in 1930, which ought to make today at least 400,000 white males of twenty-one, of whom only 250,000 vote.

Therefore, we are still all at sea, and *The Crisis* asks for information. Is it possible that the attempt of Alabama to usher in real democracy after the Tragic Era has resulted not only in the disfranchisement of all Negroes, despite the 15th Amendment, but also the disfranchisement of all white women, despite the 19th Amendment, as well as in the disfranchisement of 150,000 or more white men? If so, the net result is to put into the hands of a rump electorate of 250,000 voters, of whom 9 percent are by their own admission totally illiterate, the right to decide whether or not men like Thomas Heflin are fit to sit in the United States Senate.

1930 · vol 37

COURTS AND JAILS

It is to the disgrace of the American Negro, and particularly of his religious and philanthropic organizations, that they continually and systematically neglect Negroes who have been arrested, or who are accused of crime, or who have been convicted and incarcerated.

One can easily realize the reason for this: ever since Emancipation and even before, accused and taunted with being criminals, the emancipated and rising Negro has tried desperately to disassociate himself from his own criminal class. He has been all too eager to class criminals as outcasts, and to condemn every Negro who has the misfortune to be arrested or accused. He has joined with the bloodhounds in anathematizing every Negro in jail, and has called High Heaven to witness that he has absolutely no sympathy and no known connection with any black man who has committed crime.

All this, of course, is arrant nonsense; is a combination of ignorance and pharisaism which ought to put twelve million people to shame. There is absolutely no scientific proof, statistical, social or physical, to show that the American Negro is any more criminal than other elements in the American nation, if indeed as criminal. Moreover, even if he were, what is crime but disease, social or physical? In addition to this, every Negro knows that a frightful proportion of Negroes accused of crime are absolutely innocent. Nothing in the world is easier in the

United States than to accuse a black man of crime. In the South, if any crime is committed, the first cry of the mob is, "Find the Negro!" And while they are finding him, the white criminal comfortably escapes. Nothing is easier, South and North, than for a white man to black his face, saddle a felony upon the Negro, and then go wash his body and his soul. Today, if a Negro is accused, whether he is innocent or guilty, he not only is almost certain of conviction, but of getting the limit of the law. What else is the meaning of the extraordinary fact that throughout the United States the number of Negroes hanged, sentenced for life, or for ten, twenty or forty years, is an amazingly large proportion of the total number?

Meantime, what are we doing about it? Here and there, in a few spectacular cases, we are defending persons, where race discrimination is apparent, and where the poor devil of a victim manages to get into the newspaper. But in most cases, the whole black world is dumb and acquiescent; they will not even visit the detention houses where the accused, innocent and guilty, are herded like cattle. They make few systematic attempts to reform the juvenile delinquent who may be guilty of nothing more than energy and mischief. Only in sporadic cases do we visit the jails and hear the tales of the damned.

For a race which boasts its Christianity, and for a Church which squanders its money upon carpets, organs, stained glass, bricks and stone, this attitude toward Negro crime is the most damning accusation yet made.

1932 · vol 39

MAGNIFICAT, 1931

Blessed art thou among women and blessed is the fruit of thy womb.

And .Mary Black said: Who? Me? Blessed? and another baby coming and none of us with a job?

Blessed? How come? I can't understand you and God and I don't see no call for this soul of mine to magnify nothing! Look here: You see how we've slaved and worked and kept decent and gone to church and nobody calls us blessed —

They curse·us.

You're mighty, all right, God — I know that you've done great things and your name's holy and all that. But how about me? How about that mercy on them that was afeared of you from generation to generation? Didn't Ma and Pa serve you? Didn't Grandpa preach your Word? Ain't I tried to do right? Well, how about me, then? You got strength in your arm — you can scatter the proud — well, why don't you put down some of the mighty white folks from their seats and exalt a few black folk of low degree —

Why don't you?

Why don't you get busy when you see us hungry and cold with no money and no job? What do you do about it? I'll tell you: You fill the rich and white with good things and the poor and black you send empty away, or lynch them. You don't even help the Jews as you promised Abraham when he helped you. And now — my God! — another baby!

And the angel said:

He shall be great, and shall be called the Son of the Highest; and the Lord God shall give unto Him the throne of His father David.

The Holy Ghost shall come upon thee, and the power of the Highest shall overshadow thee; therefore also that holy thing which shall be born of thee shall be called the Son of God.

For with God nothing shall be impossible.

TO AMERICAN NEGROES
BY ALBERT EINSTEIN*

It seems to be a universal fact that minorities, especially when their individuals are recognizable because of physical differences, are treated by the majorities among whom they live as an inferior class. The tragic part of such a fate, however, lies not only in the automatically realized disadvantages suffered by these minorities in economic and social relations, but also in the fact that those who meet such treatment themselves for the most part acquiesce in this prejudiced estimate because of the suggestive influence of the majority, and come to regard people like themselves as inferior. This second and more important aspect of the evil can be met through closer union and conscious educational enlightenment among the minority, and so an emancipation of the soul of the minority can be attained.

The determined effort of the American Negroes in this direction deserves every recognition and assistance.

1932 · vol 39

EINSTEIN'S ADVICE

A Brooklyn daily paper read Einstein's "Message to Negroes" in *The Crisis*, and said:

Their racial progress has been wonderful, but the complex of inferiority dies very slowly, and the prejudices of Caucasism have equal longevity. "Blessed are the meek, for they shall inherit the earth," is probably the best method for our Negro minority.

What extraordinary advice! Under the circumstances, we would think that continued meekness on the part of

* Albert Einstein (1879—1955): International physicist

the Negro would be just about the worst possible attitude, not only for Negroes themselves, but for its effect on their white neighbors.

1932 · vol 39

LABOR "SOLIDARITY"

England has just built in Washington one of those vast estates to house the British embassy which dot the world and greatly impress it. I remember the magnificent buildings in Dakar, French West Africa, not to mention Berlin, Paris, Rome and Moscow.

The contractors wished to use some of the excellent black workers and builders of the District of Columbia who have labored on nearly all of its best buildings. But these black folk are not union men, for the simple reason that the unions, most of them affiliated with the American Federation of Labor, will neither admit Negroes nor recognize their union cards if admitted elsewhere.

Consequently, the white unions demanded "union labor" and appealed to the English Labor Party to support them. The Labor Party easily induced their representatives in the coalition government to order only "union" labor on the Washington building.

Thus, not a black man got a job.

This is another feather in Mr. MacDonald's* cap and the solidarity of American labor is correspondingly increased.

Black brothers, how would you welcome a dictatorship of this proletariat?

1932 · vol 39

* James Ramsay MacDonald: British Labor Party Prime Minister 1924; 1929—35

Race segregation in the United States too often presents itself as an individual problem; a question of my admission to this church or that theater; a question as to whether I shall live and work in Mississippi or New York for my own enjoyment, emolument or convenience.

In fact this matter of segregation is a group matter with long historic roots. When Negroes were first brought to America in any numbers, their classification was economic rather than racial. They were in law and custom classed with the laborers, most of whom were brought from Europe under a contract which made them practically serfs. In this laboring class there was at first no segregation, there was some intermarriage and when the laborer gained his freedom, he became in numbers of cases a landholder and a voter.

The first distinction arose between laborers who had come from Europe and contracted to work for a term of years, and laborers from Africa and the West Indies who had made no contract. Both classes were often held for life, but soon there arose a distinction between servants for a term of years and servants for life. Even their admission to a Christian church organization was usually considered as emancipating a servant for life, and thus again the purely racial segregation was cut across by religious considerations.

Finally, however, slavery became a matter of racial caste, so that white laborers served for definite terms and most black workers served for life. But even here anomaly arose in the case of the small number of Negroes who were free. For a while these free Negroes were not definitely segregated from other free workers, but gradually they were forced together as a caste, holding themselves, on the one hand, strictly away from the slaves, and on the other, being excluded more and more severely from intercourse with whites of all degrees.

The result was that there grew up in the minds of the free Negro class a determination and a prejudice which has come down to our day. They fought bitterly with every means at their command against being classed with the mass of slaves. It was for this reason that they objected to being called Negroes. Negroes was synonymous with slaves. They were not slaves. They objected to being coupled with black folk by legislation or custom. Any such act threatened their own freedom. They developed, therefore, both North and South as a separate, isolated group. In large Southern cities, like New Orleans, Savannah and Charleston, they organized their own society, established schools and churches, and made themselves a complete segregated unit, except in their economic relations where they earned a living among the whites as artisans and servants, rising here and there to be semiprofessional men and small merchants. The higher they rose and the more definite and effective their organization, the more they protested against being called Negroes or classed with Negroes, because Negroes were slaves.

In the North, the development differed somewhat, and yet followed mainly the same lines. The groups of free colored folk in Boston, Newport, New Haven, New York, Philadelphia, Baltimore and Cincinnati, all formed small, carefully organized groups, with their own schools and churches, with their own social life, with their own protest against being classed as Negroes. As the mass of Negroes became free in the Northern states, certain decisions were forced upon these groups. Take for instance, Philadelphia. An event happened in April, 1787, which may be called by the American Negro, the Great Decision. The free colored people of Philadelphia at that time were making a desperate fight for recognition and decent social treatment.

Two of their leaders, Richard Allen and Absalom Jones, had proffered their services during the terribly widespread epidemic and partly at their own expense helped

172

bury the deserted dead of the white folk. The Mayor properly commended them. Both these men worshipped at St. George's Methodist Church, then at 4th and Vine Streets. For years they had been made welcome; but as gradual emancipation progressed in Pennsylvania, Negroes began to pour in to the city from the surrounding country, and black Christians became too numerous at St. George's. One Sunday morning during prayer, Jones and Allen were on their knees, when they were told they must get up and go to the gallery where hereafter black folk would worship. They refused to stir until the prayer was over, and then they got up and left the church. They never went back.

Under these circumstances, what would you have done, Dear Reader of 1934? There were several possibilities. You might have been able to impress it upon the authorities of the church that you were not like other Negroes; that you were different, with more wealth and intelligence, and that while it might be quite all right and even agreeable to you that other Negroes should be sent to the gallery, that you as an old and tried member of the church should be allowed to worship as you pleased. If you had said this, it probably would have had no effect upon the deacons of St George's.

In that case, what would you have done? You could walk out of the church but whither would you walk? There were no other white churches that wanted you. Most of them would not have allowed you to cross their threshold. The others would have segregated you in the gallery or at a separate service. You might have said with full right and reason that the action of St. George's was unchristian and despicable, and dangerous for the future of democracy in Philadelphia and in the United States. That was all quite true, and nevertheless its statement had absolutely no effect upon St. George's.

Walking out of this church, these two men formed an organization. It was called the Free African Society.

Virtually it was confined to a colored membership, although some of the Quakers visited the meetings from time to time and gave advice. Probably there was some discussion of taking the group into the fellowship of the Quakers, but liberal as the Quakers were, they were not looking for Negro proselytes. They had had a few in the West Indies but not in the United States. The excluded Negroes found themselves in a dilemma. They could do one of two things: They could ask to be admitted as a segregated group·in some white organization; or they could form their own organization. It was an historic decision and they did both.

Richard Allen formed from the larger part of the group, the African Methodist Episcopal Church, which today has 750,000 members and is without doubt the most powerful single Negro organization in the United States. Absalom Jones formed St. Thomas Church as a separate Negro church in the Episcopal communion, and the church has had a continuous existence down to our day.

Which of these two methods was best will be a matter of debate. There are those who think that it was saving something of principle to remain in a white church, even as a segregated body. There are others who say that this action was simply a compromise with the devil and that having been kicked out of the Methodist Church and not allowed equality in the Episcopal Church, there was nothing for a self-respecting man to do but to establish a church of his own.

No matter which solution seems to you wisest, segregation was compulsory, and the only answer to it was internal self-organization; and the answer that was inevitable in 1787, is just as inevitable in 1934.

1934 · vol 41

Monroe Trotter was a man of heroic proportions, and probably one of the most selfless of Negro leaders during all our American history. His father was Recorder of Deeds for the District of Columbia, at the time when Recorders were paid by fees; and as a result, he retired from office with a small fortune, which he husbanded carefully.

Thus, his son was born in most comfortable circumstances, and with his talent for business, and his wide acquaintanceship with the best class of young Massachusetts men in his day, might easily have accumulated wealth.

But he turned aside. He had in his soul all that went to make a fanatic, a knight errant. Ready to sacrifice himself, fearing nobody and nothing, strong in body, sturdy in conviction, full of unbending belief.

I remember when I first saw him as a student at Harvard. He was several classes below me. I should liked to have known him and spoken to him, but he was curiously aloof. He was even then forming his philosophy of life. Colored students must not herd together, just because they were colored. He had his white friends and companions, and they liked him. He was no hanger-on, but a leader among them. But he did not seek other colored students as companions. I was a bit lonesome in those days, but I saw his point, and I did not seek him.

Out of this rose his life-long philosophy: Intense hatred of all racial discrimination and segregation. He was particularly incensed at the compromising philosophy of Booker T. Washington; at his industrialism, and his condoning of the deeds of the South.

In the first years of the twentieth century, with George Forbes, Monroe Trotter began the publication of *The Guardian*. Several times young men have started radical sheets among us, like *The Messenger*, and others. But nothing, I think, that for sheer biting invective and un-swerving courage, ever quite equaled the Boston *Guardian* in its earlier days. Mr. Washington and his followers literally shrivelled before it, and it was, of course, often as unfair as it was inspired.

I had come to know Trotter, then, especially because I knew Deenie Pindell as a girl before they were married. We were to stop with them one summer. Mrs. Du Bois was already there when I arrived in Boston, and on the elevated platform, I learned of the Zion Church riot. It was called a riot in the newspapers, and they were full of it. As a matter of fact, Trotter and Forbes had tried to ask Booker T. Washington certain pointed questions, after a speech which he made in the colored church; and im-mediately Trotter was arrested, according to careful plans which William L. Lewis, Washington's attorney, had laid. I was incensed at Trotter. I thought that he had been needlessly violent, and had compromised me as his guest; but when I learned the exact facts, and how little cause for riot there was, and when they clapped Trotter in the Charles Street Jail, all of us more conservative, younger men rose in revolt.

Out of this incident, within a year òr two, arose the Niagara movement, and Trotter was present.

But Trotter was not an organization man. He was a free lance; too intense and sturdy to loan himself to that com-promise which is the basis of all real organization. Trouble arose in the Niagara movement, and afterward when the Niagara movement joined the new NAACP, Trotter stood out in revolt, and curiously enough, did not join the new organization because of his suspicion of the white elements who were co-operating with us.

He devoted himself to *The Guardian,* and it became one of the first of the nation-wide colored weeklies. His wife worked with him in utter devotion; giving up all thought of children; giving up her pretty home in Roxbury; living and lunching with him in the *Guardian* Office, and knowing hunger and cold. It was a magnificent partnership, and she died to pay for it.

The Trotter philosophy was carried out remorselessly in his paper. He stood unflinchingly for fighting separation and discrimination in church and school, and in professional and business life. He would not allow a colored Y. M. C. A. in Boston, and he hated to recognize colored churches, or colored colleges. On this battle line he fought a long, exhausting fight for over a quarter of a century. What has been the result? There are fewer Negroes in Boston churches today than when Trotter began a crusade, and colored people sat in the pews under Phillips Brooks'* preaching. There may be more colored teachers in the schools, but certainly they are playing no such part as Maria Baldwin did, as Principal of the best Cambridge Grammar School.

When Trotter began, not a single hotel in Boston dared to refuse colored guests. Today, there are few Boston hotels where colored people are received. There is still no colored Y. M. C. A., but on the other hand, there are practically no colored members of the white "Y," and young colored men are deprived of club house and recreational facilities which they sorely need. In the professions, in general employment, and in business, there is certainly not less, and probably more discrimination than there used to be.

Does this mean that Monroe Trotter's life was a failure? Never. He lived up to his belief to the best of his ability. He fought like a man. The ultimate object of his fighting was absolutely right, but he miscalculated the opposition. He thought that Boston and America would yield to clear reason and determined agitation. They did not. On the contrary, to some extent, the very agitation carried on in these years has solidified opposition. This does not mean

* Phillips Brooks (1835—93): U.S. Protestant Episcopal Bishop and pulpit orator

that agitation does not pay; but it means that you cannot necessarily cash in quickly upon it. It means that sacrifice, even to blood and tears, must be given to this great fight; and not one but a thousand lives, like that of Monroe Trotter, is necessary to victory.

More than that, inner organization is demanded. The free lance like Trotter is not strong enough. The mailed fist has got to be clenched. The united effort of twelve millions has got to be made to mean more than the individual effort of those who think aright. Yet this very inner organization involves segregation. It involves voluntary racial organization, and this racial grouping invites further effort at enforced segregation by law and custom from without. Nevertheless, there is no alternative. We have got to unite to save ourselves, and while the unbending devotion to principle, such as Monroe Trotter shows, has and must ever have, its value, with sorrow, and yet with conviction, we know that this is not enough.

I can understand his death. I can see a man of sixty, tired and disappointed, facing poverty and defeat. Standing amid indifferent friends and triumphant enemies. So he went to the window of his Dark Tower, and beckoned to Death; up from where She lay among the lilies. And Death, like a whirlwind, swept up to him. I shall think of him as lying silent, cold and still; at last at peace, dreamless and serene. Let no trump of doom disturb him from his perfect and eternal rest.

1934 · vol 41

A MISCELLANY OF POETRY
AND PROSE

Considered the Dean of American Negro
letters because of his erudition, his literary talent as well as his concern for the
humanities, Dr. Du Bois has published a
large body of works: novels, stories, po-
etry — reportages, speeches and books on
sociology. In them is reflected the American scene in all its reality: harsh, bare,
violent; its dark side often accented —
yet never without the hope for its bright
and better future. With warmth and humor,
with biting satire and anger at injustice,
Dr. Du Bois has written what has needed to
be said to white Americans of their black
brothers. A few excerpts of these writings
are included in the section which follows

THE WHITE MAN'S BURDEN

The author published in November, 1914, his despair at efforts to settle the race problems:

Until the Black Christ be Born!

Dark daughter of the lotus leaves that watch the
    Southern sea,
Wan spirit of a prisoned soul a-panting to be free;
    The muttered music of thy streams, the whispers of
    the deep
    Have kissed each other in God's name and kissed a
    world to sleep.

The will of the world is a whistling wind sweeping a
    cloud-cast sky,
And not from the east and not from the west knelled its
    soul-searing cry;
But out of the past of the Past's gray past, it yelled from
    the top of the sky;
    Crying: Awake, O ancient race! Wailing: O woman
    arise!
    And crying and sighing and crying again as a voice
    in the midnight cries;
    But the burden of white men bore her back, and the
    white world stifled her sighs.

The White World's vermin and filth:
    All the dirt of London,
    All the scum of New York;
    Valiant spoilers of women
    And conquerors of unarmed men;
    Shameless breeders of bastards
    Drunk with the greed of gold,
    Baiting their blood-stained hooks
    With cant for the souls of the simple,

Bearing the White Man's Burden
Of Liquor and Lust and Lies!
Unthankful we wince in the East,
Unthankful we wail from the westward,
Unthankfully thankful we sing,
In the un-won wastes of the wild:
     I hate them, Oh!
     I hate them well,
     I hate them, Christ!
     As I hate Hell,
     If I were God
     I'd sound their knell
     This day!

Who raised the fools to their glory
But black men of Egypt and Ind?
Ethiopia's sons of the evening,
Chaldeans and Yellow Chinese?
The Hebrew children of Morning
And mongrels of Rome and Greece?
     Ah, well!

And they that raised the bastards
Shall drag them down again:
Down with the theft of their thieving
And murder and mocking of men,
Down with their barter of women
And laying and lying of creeds,
Down with their cheating of childhood,
And drunken orgies of war —

    down,

      down,

        deep down,

Till the Devil's strength be shorn,
Till some dim, darker David a-hoeing of his corn,

And married maiden, Mother of God,
Bid the Black Christ be born!

Then shall the burden of manhood,
Be it yellow or black or white,
And Poverty, Justice and Sorrow —
The Humble and Simple and Strong,
Shall sing with the Sons of Morning
And Daughters of Evensong:

Black mother of the iron hills that guard the blazing sea,
Wild spirit of a storm-swept soul a-struggling to be free,
Where 'neath the bloody finger marks, thy riven bosom
    quakes,
Thicken the thunders of man's voice, and lo!
    a world awakes!

The Crisis: 1914 · vol 9

THE EXILE

August, 1923

Summer is come with bursting flower and promise of perfect fruit. Rain is rolling down Nile and Niger. Summer sings on the sea where giant ships carry busy worlds, while mermaids swarm the shores. Earth is pregnant. Life is big with pain and evil and hope. Summer in blue New York; summer in gray Berlin; summer in the red heart of the world!

I

Matthew Towns was in a cold white fury. He stood on the deck of the *Orizaba* looking down on the flying sea. In the night America had disappeared and now there was nothing but waters heaving in the bright morning. There were many passengers walking, talking, laughing; but none of them spoke to Matthew. They spoke about him, noting his tall, lean form and dark brown face, the stiff, curled mass of hair, and the midnight of his angry eyes.

They spoke about him, and he was acutely conscious of every word. Each word heard and unheard pierced him and quivered in the quick. Yet he leaned stiff and grim, gazing into the sea, his back toward all. He saw the curled grace of the billows, the changing blues and greens; and he saw, there at the edge of the world, certain shining shapes that leapt and played.

Then they changed — always they changed; and there arose the great cool height of the room at the University of Manhattan. Again he stood before the walnut rail that separated student and Dean. Again he felt the bewilderment, the surge of hot surprise.

"I cannot register at all for obstetrics?"

"No," said the Dean quietly, his face growing red. "I'm sorry, but the committee —"

"But — but — why, I'm Towns. I've already finished two years — I've ranked my class. I took honors — why — I — This is my Junior year — I must —"

He was sputtering with amazement.

"I'm sorry."

"Hell! I'm not asking your pity, I'm demanding —"

The Dean's lips grew thin and hard, and he sent the shaft home as if to rid himself quickly of a hateful task.

"Well — what did you expect? Juniors must have obstetrical work. Do you think white women patients are going to have a nigger doctor delivering their babies?"

Then Matthew's fury had burst its bounds; he had thrown his certificates, his marks and commendations straight into the drawn white face of the Dean and stumbled out. He came out on Broadway with its wide expanse, and opposite a little park. He turned and glanced up at the gray piles of tan buildings, threatening the sky, which were the University's great medical center. He stared at them. Then with bowed head he plunged down

165th Street. The gray-blue Hudson lay beneath his feet, and above it piled the Palisades upward in gray and green. He walked and walked: down the curving drive between high homes and the Hudson; by graveyard and palace; tomb and restaurant; beauty and smoke. All the afternoon he walked, all night, and into the gray dawn of another morning.

II

In after years when Matthew looked back upon this first sea voyage, he remembered it chiefly as the time of sleep; of days of long, long rest and thought, after work and hurry and rage. He was indeed very tired. A year of the hardest kind of study had been followed by a summer as clerical assistant in a colored industrial insurance office, in the heat of Washington. Thence he had hurried straight to the university with five hundred dollars of tuition money in his pocket; and now he was sailing to Europe.

Excerpt: DARK PRINCESS (N. Y., Harcourt, Brace & World, Inc., 1928)

ON GROWING OLD

I have been favored among the majority of men in never being compelled to earn my bread and butter by doing work that was uninteresting or which I did not enjoy or of the sort in which I did not find my greatest life interest. This rendered me so content in my vocation that I seldom thought about salary or haggled over it. My first job paid me eight hundred dollars a year and to take it I refused one which offered ten hundred and fifty. I served over a year at the University of Pennsylvania for the munificent sum of six hundred dollars and never railed at fate. I taught and worked at Atlanta University for twelve hundred a year during thirteen effective and happy years. I never once asked for an increase. I went to New York for the salary offered and only asked for an increase there when an efficient new white secretary was hired at a wage above mine. I then asked equal salary. I did not want the shadow of racial discrimination to creep into our salary schedule.

I realize now that this rather specious monetary independence may in the end cost me dearly, and land me in time upon some convenient street corner with a tin cup. For I have saved nearly nothing and lost my life insurance in the depression. Nevertheless, I insist that regardless of income, work worth while which one wants to do as compared with highly paid drudgery is exactly the difference between heaven and hell.

I am especially glad of the divine gift of laughter; it has made the world human and lovable, despite all its pain and wrong. I am glad that the partial Puritanism of my upbringing has never made me afraid of life. I have lived completely, testing every normal appetite, feasting on sunset, sea and hill, and enjoying wine, women, and song. I have seen the face of beauty from the Grand Canyon to the great Wall of China; from the Alps to Lake Baikal; from the African bush to the Venus of Milo.

Perhaps above all I am proud of a straightforward clearness of reason, in part a gift of the gods, but also to no little degree due to scientific training and inner discipline. By means of this I have met life face to face, I have loved a fight and I have realized that Love is God and Work is His prophet; that His ministers are Age and Death.

This makes it the more incomprehensible for me to see persons quite panic-stricken at the approach of their thirtieth birthday and prepared for dissolution at forty. Few of my friends have openly celebrated their fiftieth birthdays, and near none their sixtieth. Of course, one sees some reasons: the disappointment at meager accomplishment which all of us to some extent share; the haunting shadow of possible decline; the fear of death. I have been fortunate in having health and wise in keeping it. I have never shared what seems to me the essentially childish desire to live forever. Life has its pain and evil — its bitter disappointments; but I like a good novel and in healthful length of days, there is infinite joy in seeing the World, the most interesting of continued stories, unfold, even though one misses *the end.*

Excerpt: DUSK OF DAWN (N. Y., Harcourt, Brace & World, Inc., 1940)

THE WAR TO PRESERVE HUMAN SLAVERY

One hundred years ago this nation fought a civil war to preserve Negro slavery in the Southern states, prevent its spread into the North and yet keep the nation unified so that it could control the cotton crop which slaves raised. Negro slaves played a vital part in this war and indeed its result was their emancipation, which as Lincoln said could not have been accomplished without their aid. Du Bois wrote Black Reconstruction, *"An essay toward a history of the part which black folk played in the attempt to reconstruct democracy in America." An excerpt from that book follows.*

NEGRO TROOPS

It had been a commonplace thing in the North to declare that Negroes would not fight. Even the black man's friends were skeptical about the possibility of using him as a soldier, and far from its being to the credit of black men, or any men, that they did not want to kill, the ability and willingness to take human life has always been, even in the minds of liberal men, a proof of manhood. It took in many respects a finer type of courage for the Negro to work quietly and faithfully as a slave while the world was fighting over his destiny, than it did to seize a bayonet and rush mad with fury or inflamed with drink, and plunge it into the bowels of a stranger. Yet this was the proof of manhood required of the Negro. He might plead his cause with the tongue of Frederick Douglass, and the nation listened almost unmoved. He might labor for the nation's wealth, and the nation took the results without thanks, and handed him as near nothing in return as would keep him alive. He was called a coward and a fool when he protected the women and children of his master. But when he rose and fought and killed, the whole nation with one voice proclaimed him a man and brother. Nothing else made emancipation possible in the United States. Nothing else made Negro citizenship conceivable, but the record of the Negro soldier as a fighter.

The military aid of Negroes began as laborers and spies.

A soldier said: "This war has been full of records of Negro agency in our behalf. Negro guides have piloted our forces; Negro sympathy cared for our prisoners escaping from the enemy; Negro hands have made for us naval captures; Negro spies brought us valuable information. The Negroes of the South have been in sympathy with us from the beginning, and have always hailed the approach of our flag with the wildest demonstrations of joy."

All through the war and after, Negroes were indispensable as informers, as is well known. The Southern papers had repeated notices of the work of Negro spies. In Richmond, a white woman with dispatches for the Confederate army was arrested in 1863 on information given by a Negro. At the Battle of Manassas, the house of a free Negro was used as a refuge for the dead and wounded Union men. Negro pilots repeatedly guided Federal boats in Southern waters, and there were several celebrated cases of whole boats being seized by Negro pilots. A typical instance of this type was the action of William F. Tillman, a colored steward on board the brig *S. J. Waring,* which carried a cargo valued at $100,000. He had succeeded, by leading a revolt, in freeing the vessel from the Confederates who had seized it, and with the aid of a German and a Canadian had brought the vessel into port at New York. This action brought up the question of whether a Negro could be master of a vessel. In the Official Opinions of the Attorney-General for 1862, it was declared that a free colored man if born in the United States was a citizen of the United States and was competent to be master of a vessel engaged in the coasting trade.

The case of Smalls* and the *Planter* at Charleston, South Carolina, became almost classic. "While at the wheel of the *Planter* as Pilot in the rebel service, it occurred to me that I could not only secure my own freedom, but that of numbers of my comrades in bonds, and moreover, I thought the *Planter* might be of some use to Uncle Abe. . . .

"I reported my plans for rescuing the *Planter* from the rebel captain to the crew (all colored), and secured their secrecy and co-operation.

"On May 13, 1862, we took on board several large guns at the Atlantic Dock. At evening of that day, the Captain went home, leaving the boat in my care, with instruction to send for him in case he should be wanted. . . . At half-past three o'clock on the morning of the 14th of May, I left the Atlantic Dock with the *Planter,* went to the *Ettaoue;* took on board my family; and several other families, then proceeded down Charleston River slowly. When opposite . . . Fort Sumter at 4 a. m., I gave the signal, which was answered from the Fort, thereby giving permission

* Robert Smalls (1839—1915): Served in the U. S. Congress, 1875—87, a longer period than any other Negro of his time

to pass. I then made speed for the Blockading Fleet. When entirely out of range of Sumter's guns, I hoisted a white flag, and at 5 a. m., reached a U.S. blockading vessel . . ."

Negro military labor had been indispensable to the Union armies. "Negroes built most of the fortifications and earth-works for General Grant in front of Vicksburg. The works in and about Nashville were cast up by the strong arm and willing hand of the loyal Blacks. Dutch Gap was dug by Negroes, and miles of earth-works, fortifications, and corduroy-roads were made by Negroes. They did fatigue duty in every department of the Union army. Wherever a Negro appeared with a shovel in his hand, a white soldier took his gun and returned to the ranks. There were 200,000 Negroes in the camps and employ of the Union armies, as servants, teamsters, cooks, and laborers."

The South was for a long time convinced that the Negro could not and would not fight. "The idea of their doing any serious fighting against white men is simply ridiculous," said an editorial in the Savannah *Republican*, March 25, 1863.

Of the actual fighting of Negroes, a Union general, Morgan, afterward interested in Negro education, says:

"History has not yet done justice to the share borne by colored soldiers in the war for the Union. Their conduct during that eventful period, has been a silent, but most potent factor in influencing public sentiment, shaping legislation, and fixing the status of colored people in America. If the records of their achievements could be accessible to the thousands of colored youth in the South, they would kindle in their young minds an enthusiastic devotion to manhood and liberty."

Black men were repeatedly and deliberately used as shock troops, when there was little or no hope of success. In February, 1863, Colonel Thomas Wentworth Higginson led black troops into Florida, and said: "It would have been madness to attempt with the bravest white troops what was successfully accomplished with black ones."

In April, there were three white companies from Maine and seven Negro companies on Ship Island, the key to New Orleans. The black troops with black officers were attacked by Confederates who outnumbered them five to one. The Negroes retreated so as to give the Federal gunboat *Jackson* a chance to shell their pursuers. But the white crew disliked the Negro soldiers, and opened fire directly upon the black troops while they were fighting the Confederates. Major Dumas, the Negro officer in command, rescued the black men; repulsed the Confederates, and brought the men out safely. The commander called attention to these colored officers: "They were constantly in the thickest of the fight, and by their unflinching bravery, and admirable handling of their commands, contributed to the success of the attack, and reflected great honor upon the flag."

The first battle with numbers of Negro troops followed soon after. Banks laid siege to Port Hudson with all his forces, including two black regiments. On May 23, 1863, the assault was ordered, but the various co-operating organizations did not advance simultaneously. The Negro regiments, on the North, made three desperate charges, losing heavily, but maintained the advance over a field covered with recently felled trees. Confederate batteries opened fire upon them. Michigan, New York and Massachusetts white troops were hurled back, but the works had to be taken. Two Negro regiments were ordered to go forward, through a direct and cross fire.

"The deeds of heroism performed by these colored men were such as the proudest white men might emulate. Their colors are torn to pieces by shot, and literally bespattered by blood and brains. The color-sergeant of the 1st Louisiana, on being mortally wounded, hugged the colors to his breast, when a struggle ensued between the two color-corporals on each side of him, as to who should have the honor of bearing the sacred standard, and during this generous contention, one was seriously wounded. One black lieutenant actually mounted the enemy's works three or four times, and in one charge the assaulting party came within fifty paces of them. Indeed, if only ordinarily supported by artillery and reserve, no one can convince us that they would not have opened a passage through the enemy's works.

"Captain Callioux of the 1st Louisiana, a man so black that he actually prided himself upon his blackness, died the death of a hero, leading on his men in the thickest of the fight.

"Lieutenant-Colonel Bassett being driven back, Colonel Finnegas took his place, and his men being similarly cut to pieces, Bassett reformed and recommenced; and thus these brave people went on, from morning until 3:30 p. m., under the most hideous carnage that men ever had to withstand, and that very few white ones would have had nerve to encounter, even if ordered to. During this time, they rallied, and *were ordered to make six distinct charges,* losing thirty-seven killed, and one hundred and fifty-five wounded, and one hundred and sixteen missing — the majority, if not all, of these being in all probability, now lying dead on the gory field, and without the rites of sepulture; for when, by flag of truce, our forces in other direction were permitted to reclaim their dead, the benefit, through some neglect, was not extended to these black regiments!"

In June, came the battle of Milliken's Bend. Grant,* in order to capture Vicksburg, had drawn nearly all his troops from Milliken's Bend, except three Negro regiments, and a small force of white cavalry. This force was surprised by the Confederates, who drove the white cavalry to the very breastworks of the fort. Here the

* Ulysses S. Grant: Union General; later 18th President of the United States, 1869—77

Confederates rested, expecting to take the fortifications in the morning. At three o'clock, they rushed over with drawn bayonets, but the Negroes drove them out of the forts and held them until the gunboats came up. One officer describes the fight:

"Before the colonel was ready, the men were in line, ready for action. As before stated, the rebels drove our force toward the gunboats, taking colored men prisoners and murdering them. This so enraged them that they rallied, and charged the enemy more heroically and desperately than has been recorded during the war. It was a genuine bayonet charge, a hand-to-hand fight, that has never occurred to any extent during this prolonged conflict. Upon both sides men were killed with the butts of muskets. White and black men were lying side by side, pierced by bayonets, and in some instances transfixed to the earth. In one instance, two men, one white and the other black, were found dead, side by side, each having the other's bayonet through his body. If facts prove to be what they are now represented, this engagement of Sunday morning will be recorded as the most desperate of this war. Broken limbs, broken heads, the mangling of bodies, all prove that it was a contest between enraged men: on the one side from hatred to a race; and on the other, desire for self-preservation, revenge for past grievances and the inhuman murder of their comrades."

The month of July, 1863, was memorable. General Meade* had driven Lee** from Gettysburg, Grant had captured Vicksburg, Banks* had captured Port Hudson, and Gilmore* had begun his operations on Morris Island. On the 13th of July, the draft riot broke out in New York City, and before it was over, a Negro regiment in South Carolina, the 54th Massachusetts, was preparing to lead the assault on Fort Wagner. It was a desperate, impossible

* Meade, Banks, Gilmore: Officers in the Union Army
** Robert E. Lee: Confederate Commander-in-Chief

venture, which failed, but can never be forgotten. The black Fifty-Fourth Massachusetts regiment was to lead the assault.

"Wagner loomed, black, grim and silent. There was no glimmer of light. Nevertheless, in the fort, down below the level of the tide, and under roofs made by huge trunks of trees, lay two thousand Confederate soldiers hidden. Our troops advanced toward the fort, while our mortars in the rear tossed bombs over their heads. Behind the 54th came five regiments from Connecticut, New York, New Hampshire, Pennsylvania and Maine. The mass went quickly and silently in the night. Then, suddenly, the walls of the fort burst with a blinding sheet of vivid light. Shot, shells of iron and bullets crushed through the dense masses of the attacking force. I shall never forget the terrible sound of that awful blast of death which swept down, battered or dead, a thousand of our men. Not a shot had missed its aim. Every bolt of iron and lead tasted of human blood.

"The column wavered ·and recovered itself. They reached the ditch before the fort. They climbed on the ramparts and swarmed over the walls. It looked as though the fort was captured. Then there came another blinding blaze from concealed guns in the rear of the fort, and the men went down by scores. The rebels rallied, and were reenforced by thousands of others, who had landed on the beach in the darkness unseen by the fleet. They hurled themselves upon the attacking force. The struggle was terrific. The supporting units hurried up to aid their comrades, but as they raised the ramparts, they fired a volley which struck down many of their own men. Our men rallied again, but were forced back to the edge of the ditch. Colonel Shaw, with scores of his black fighters, went down struggling desperately. Resistance was vain. The assailants were forced back to the beach, and the rebels drilled their recovered cannons anew on the remaining survivors."

When a request was made for Colonel Shaw's body, a Confederate Major said: "We have buried him with his niggers."

In December, 1863, Morgan led Negro troops in the battle of Nashville. He declared a new chapter in the history of liberty had been written. "It had been shown that marching under a flag of freedom, animated by a love of liberty, even the slave becomes a man and a hero." Between eight and ten thousand Negro troops took part in the battles around Nashville, all of them from slave states.

When General Thomas* rode over the battlefield, and saw the bodies of colored men side by side with the foremost on the very works of the enemy, he turned to his staff, saying: "Gentlemen, the question is settled: Negroes will fight."

How extraordinary, and what a tribute to ignorance and religious hypocrisy, is the fact that in the minds of most people, even those of liberals, only murder makes men. The slave pleaded; he was humble; he protected the women of the South, and the world ignored him. The slave killed white men; and behold, he was a man!

The *New York Times* said conservatively, in 1863:

Negro soldiers have now been in battle at Port Hudson and at Milliken's Bend in Louisiana, at Helena in Arkansas, at Morris Island in South Carolina, and at or near Fort Gibson in the Indian territory. In two of these instances they assaulted fortified positions, and led the assault; in two, they fought on the defensive, and in one, they attacked rebel infantry. In all of them, they acted in conjunction with white troops, and under command of white officers. In some instances, they acted with distinguished bravery, and in all, they acted as well as could be expected of raw troops.

* George Henry Thomas: Union General

Even the *New York Herald* wrote in May, 1864:

The conduct of the colored troops, by the way, in the actions of the last few days, is described as superb. An Ohio soldier said to me today, "I never saw men fight with such desperate gallantry as those Negroes did. They advanced as grim and stern as death, and when within· reach of the enemy struck about them with pitiless vigor, that was almost fearful." Another soldier said to me: "These Negroes never shrink, nor hold back, no matter what the order. Through scorching heat and pelting storms, if the order comes, they march with prompt, ready feet." Such praise is great praise, and it is deserved.

And there was a significant dispatch in the *New York Tribune* July 26th:

In speaking of the soldierly qualities of our colored troops, I do not refer especially to their noble action in the perilous edge of the battle; that is settled, but to their docility and their patience of labor and suffering in the camp and on the march.

Grant was made Lieutenant-General in 1864, and began to reorganize the armies. When he came East, he found that few Negro troops had been used in Virginia. He therefore transferred nearly twenty thousand Negroes from the Southern and Western armies to the army of Virginia. They fought in nearly all the battles around Petersburg and Richmond, and officers on the field reported:

"The problem is solved. The Negro is a man, a soldier, a hero. Knowing of your laudable interest in the colored troops, but particularly those raised under the immediate auspices of the Supervisory Committee, I have thought it proper that I should let you know how they acquitted themselves in the late actions in front of Petersburg, of which you have already received newspaper accounts. If you remember, in my conversations upon the character of these troops, I carefully avoided saying anything about their fighting qualities till I could have an opportunity of trying them."

When the siege of Petersburg began, there were desperate battles the 16th, 17th and 18th of June. The presence of Negro soldiers rendered the enemy especially spiteful, and there were continual scrimmages and sharp shooting. Burnside's* 9th Corps had a brigade of black troops, who advanced within fifty yards of the enemy works. There was a small projecting fort which it was decided to mine and destroy.

The colored troops were to charge after the mine was set off. An inspecting officer reported that the "black corps was fittest for the perilous services," but Meade objected to colored troops leading the assault. Burnside insisted. The matter was referred to Grant, and he agreed with Meade. A white division led the assault and failed. The battle of the Crater followed.

Captain McCabe says: "It was now eight o'clock in the morning. The rest of Potter's (Federal) division moved out slowly, when Ferrero's Negro division, the men beyond question, inflamed with drink (There are many officers and men, myself among the number, who will testify to this), burst from the advanced lines, cheering vehemently, passed at a double quick over a crest under a heavy fire, and rushed with scarcely a check over the heads of the white troops in the crater, spread to their right, and captured more than 200 prisoners and one stand of colors."

General Grant afterward said: "General Burnside wanted to put his colored troops in front. I believe if he had done so, it would have been a success."

The following spring, April 3rd, the Federal troops entered Richmond. Weitzel was leading, with a black

* Ambrose Everett Burnside: Union General

196

regiment in his command — a long blue line with gun-barrels gleaming, and bands playing: *John Brown's body lies a-moldering in the grave but his soul goes marching on.*

President Lincoln visited the city after the surrender, and the Connecticut colored troops, known as the 29th Colored Regiment, witnessed his entry. One member of this unit said:

"When the President landed, there was no carriage near, neither did he wait for one, but leading his son, they walked over a mile to General Weitzel's headquarters at Jeff Davis'* mansion, a colored man acting as guide. . . . What a spectacle! I never witnessed such rejoicing in all my life. As the President passed along the street, the colored people waved their handkerchiefs, hats and bonnets, and expressed their gratitude by shouting repeatedly, 'Thank God for His goodness; we have seen His salvation.' . . .

"No wonder tears came to his eyes, when he looked on the poor colored people who were once slaves, and heard the blessings uttered from thankful hearts and thanksgiving to God and Jesus. . . . After visiting Jefferson Davis' mansion, he proceeded to the rebel capitol, and from the steps delivered a short speech, and spoke to the colored people, as follows:

" 'In reference to you, colored people, let me say, God has made you free. Although you have been deprived of your God-given rights by your so-called masters, you are now as free as I am, and if those that claim to be your superiors do not know that you are free, take the sword and bayonet and teach them that you are — for God created all men free, giving to each the same rights of life, liberty and the pursuit of happiness.' "

The recruiting of Negro soldiers was hastened after the

* Jefferson Davis: President of the Confederate States of America, 1861—65

battle of Fort Wagner, until finally no less than 154 regiments, designated as United States Negro troops, were enlisted. They included 140 infantry regiments, seven cavalry regiments, 13 artillery regiments, and 11 separate companies and batteries. The whole number enlisted will never be accurately known, since in the Department of the Gulf and elsewhere, there was a practice of putting a living Negro soldier in a dead one's place under the same name.

Official figures say that there were in all 186,017 Negro troops, of whom 123,156 were still in service, July 16, 1865; and that the losses during the war were 68,178. They took part in 198 battles and skirmishes. Without doubt, including servants, laborers and spies, between three and four hundred thousand Negroes helped as regular soldiers or laborers in winning the Civil War.

The world knows that noble inscription on St. Gaudens' Shaw Monument in Boston Common written by President Eliot:

THE WHITE OFFICERS

Taking Life and Honor in their Hands — Cast their Lot with Men of a Despised Race Unproved in War — and Risked Death as Inciters of a Servile Insurrection if Taken Prisoners, Besides Encountering all the Common Perils of Camp, March and Battle.

Excerpt: BLACK RECONSTRUCTION (N. Y., Harcourt, Brace & World, Inc., 1935)

THE COLD WAR

1946—1958 ... When Dr. Du Bois was approaching the eighth decade of his life the cold war was in its infancy. That his long years of work did not permit a letup in his activities, both in the political field and in the field of writing, is perhaps the most remarkable aspect of a distinguished career.. The excerpts contained in this section concern his participation in questions of the day: desegregation in the United States, the road of the new nations arising in Africa, the cold war and above all the question of war or peace...

BEHOLD THE LAND

At the closing public session of the Southern Youth Legislature, eight hundred and sixty-one young delegates Negro and white, crowded into Antisdel Chapel of Benedict College in Columbia, South Carolina. They were joined by a large and sympathetic public who stood in the aisles, jammed the doors and listened through loudspeakers outside the auditorium. They had come to hear the address of Du Bois which follows.

The future of American Negroes is in the South. Here three hundred and twenty-seven years ago, they began to enter what is now the United States of America; here they have suffered the damnation of slavery, the frustration of reconstruction and the lynching of emancipation. I trust then that an organization like yours is going to regard the South as the battleground of a great crusade. Here is the magnificent climate; here is the fruitful earth under the beauty of the Southern sun; and here if anywhere on earth, is the need of the thinker, the worker and the dreamer. This is the firing line not simply for the emancipation of the American Negro but for the emancipation of the African Negro and the Negroes of the West Indies; for the emancipation of the colored races; and for the emancipation of the white slaves of modern capitalistic monopoly.

White youth in the South is peculiarly frustrated. There is not a single great ideal which they can express or aspire to, that does not bring them into flat contradiction with the Negro problem. The more they try to escape it, the more they land into hypocrisy, lying and double-dealing; the more they become, what they least wish to become, the oppressors and despisers of human beings. Some of them, in larger and larger numbers, are bound to turn toward the truth and to recognize you as brothers and as sisters, and as fellow travelers toward the new dawn.

Nevertheless reason can and will prevail; but of course it can only prevail with publicity — pitiless, blatant publicity. You have got to make the people of the United States and of the world know what is going on in the South. You have got to use every field of publicity to force the truth into their ears, and before their eyes. You have got to make it impossible for any human being to live in the South and not realize the barbarities that prevail here. You may be condemned for flamboyant methods; for calling a congress like this; for waving your grievances under the noses and in the faces of men. That makes no difference; it is your duty to do it. It is your duty to do more of this sort of thing than you have done in the past. As a result of this you are going to be called upon for sacrifice. It is no easy thing for a young black man or a young black woman to live in the South today and to plan to continue to live here; to marry and raise children; to establish a home. They are in the midst of legal caste and customary insults; they are in continuous danger of mob violence; they are mistreated by the officers of the law and they have no hearing before the courts and the churches and public opinion commensurate with the attention which they ought to receive. But that sacrifice is only the Beginning of Battle. You must rebuild this South.

There are enormous opportunities here for a new nation, a new economy, a new culture in a South really new and not a mere renewal of an old South of slavery, monopoly and race hatred. There is a chance for a new co-operative agriculture on renewed land owned by the State with capital furnished by the State, mechanized and co-ordinated with city life. There is a chance for strong, virile trade unions without race discrimination, with high wage, closed shop and decent conditions of work, to beat back and hold in check the swarm of landlords, monop- olists and profiteers who are today sucking the blood out of this land. There is a chance for co-operative industry, built on the cheap power of T.V.A.* and its future extensions. There is opportunity to organize and mechanize domestic service with decent hours, and high wages and dignified training.

Excerpt: *Behold The Land*, Birmingham 1946

AT MADISON SQUARE GARDEN

On May 13, 1952, at Madison Square Garden in New York City, Dr. Du Bois gave the keynote address at a meeting sponsored by the American Labor Party which launched its 1952 campaign for the office of President of the U.S.A. Seventeen thousand persons attended. The text follows.

What is wrong with the United States? We are an intelligent, rich and powerful nation. Yet today we are confused and frightened. We fear poverty, unemployment and jail.

We are suspicious not only of enemies but especially of friends. We shrink before the world and are ready to make war on everybody. General Eisenhower has assured us that "we can lick the world" and we are preparing to spend billions of dollars to do it even when we do not know whom to fight or why or how.

Of the thirty-five civilized nations of the world, we and Japan are the only ones which have refused to sign the International Treaty promising not to resort to germ warfare; and it is widely charged that we are now using bacteria in China.

* T.V.A.: Tennessee Valley Authority, government-owned power project harnessing the Tennessee River

We face today a national election, to exercise the greatest prerogative of citizenship, in order to decide our future policy as to peace and war; trade and commerce; taxation, wages and prices; employment; social progress in housing, flood control, education, sickness and old age; honesty in public service; labor unions and civil rights.

These are tremendous problems before us which we are supposed to settle in broad outline, and yet apparently we will not have real opportunity to pass judgment on these questions.

We are deprived from day to day of knowledge of the real facts. Our sons fight and die and we cannot learn why or how. Deaths by bullets are reported but deaths by freezing and disease are concealed. We are allowed no free discussion on platform or over the radio; in newspapers or periodicals. Nearly every independent thinker has been silenced, while stool pigeons, traitors and professed liars picked by wealth, industry and power, can talk to the nation unhampered and ungagged.

We know that the nation is spending far more money than it is collecting or can collect, and that rising prices, pushed by huge private profits, are putting the cost of living ever beyond a decent standard of living for most of us. Our industry and continued employment depend largely on foreign trade, yet we are stopping foreign trade by cutting down imports and refusing to buy the goods we need from the nations who want to sell. Unless we continue to make weapons and war our economy may utterly collapse. Continually prices are outrunning wages, yet union labor, led too often by reactionary stupid men, is under increasing and co-ordinated attack, and its energies dissipated by internal division. We are spending millions on misleading advertising to increase private profit in patent medicines, toothpaste and junk. We are faced by increasing graft and stealing and lying in high office, and the highest office is afraid to investigate lest we know the thieves by name.

We are no longer free to travel, to speak our minds.
We are money-mad. Greed and wealth have chained the
beast of power. Yet, as my dead schoolmate once sang:

> *The beast said in his breast*
> *Till the mills I grind have ceased*
> *The riches shall be dust of dust*
> *Dry ashes be the feast.*

What can we do about it? How can we face and heal
our plight? Not by silence, not by fear; not by voting again
for the same old parties and going continually over the
same mumbo jumbo of meaningless elections. We are
boasting we are free when we are not free even to cast
our ballots. We are peddling freedom to the world and
daring them to oppose it and bribing them kindly to accept it, and dropping death on those who refuse it; while
we, the real victims, whose taxes furnish the bribes and
whose dead and crippled and insane children furnish the
soldiers, sit and ask with vacant faces: for whom shall we
vote, which candidate shall we vote for, and if you please,
dear candidate — will you kindly please tell us: What the
hell do you stand for anyway? Is it too much for us to ask
of your Majesty?

Yet we are fooling nobody, not even ourselves. We have
no choice. There are no two parties. There is no choice of
candidates whether his name is Eisenhower* or Taft,
Kefauver or Stassen or Warren, Dulles or Dewey, Joe or
Charlie McCarthy.** All of them listen to their master's
voice, the steel trust, the aluminium trust, the rubber com-
bine, the automobile industry; oil, power, plastics, the
railroads, tobacco, copper, chemicals and coca-cola, tele-

---

*Dwight D. Eisenhower, Taft, Kefauver, Stassen, Warren,
Dulles, Dewey: Candidates of the Democratic and Republican
Parties for political office
** Joseph McCarthy: notorious, reactionary Congressman;
Charlie McCarthy: a ventriloquist dummy, famous on radio

graph and telephone; liquor, radio and movie — all of the
more than two hundred giant corporations which wield
the power that owns the press and the magazines, and
determines what news the news agencies will print, and
what the movies will screen. They are united in that super-
congress of which the National Association of Manufac-
turers is the upper house and the United States Chamber
of Commerce is the lower, which are preparing world war
to rule mankind and reduce again the worker not simply
to slavery but to idiocy.

Address: *At Maatson Square Garden,* 1952

LET'S RESTORE DEMOCRACY TO AMERICA

To your tents, Americans! We have gone far enough into
this morass of fear, war, hate, lying and crime. We face a
crisis and our first great duty is here and now.

For the time being, never mind the Soviet Union; forget China; ignore Germany!

Come back home and look at America.

Come back to the problem of American Negroes which
we have muddled over for three hundred years.

In 1655 Spain laid plans for bringing to America three
thousand black men from Africa each year. The colonizers
ignored Las Casas who worked for the abolition of slavery
in Spanish America, and knighted John Hawkins in his
slave ship, called the *Jesus.*

In 1755, new, free America held 300,000 black folk,
nearly a fourth of the total population, in human slavery;
we ignored Milton, Baxter and Burke* and refused to
stop the African slave trade.

---

* John Milton (1608—74); Richard Baxter (1615—91); Ed-
mund Burke (1729—97); British statesmen and authors

In 1855, the Supreme Court was about to declare that Negroes had no rights which a white man was bound to respect; and the South was ready to risk Civil War to make slave territory of the whole United States.

There followed a century of war, violence and Color Caste, until the nation ashamed, started back toward Democracy. Lynching reached a climax and declined; Negroes were disfranchised and then began to vote and hold office; Negro education increased, but not as fast as it should. In 1954, the Supreme Court declared race segregation in public education was unconstitutional.

In 1955, murder, violence and economic repression began to increase, especially in Mississippi, and also widely throughout that part of the nation which once fought for human slavery and long refused to obey the Thirteenth, Fourteenth and Fifteenth Amendments* to the Constitution. Southern governors and United States senators threatened to nullify the unanimous decision of the Supreme Court.

What are we going to do about it? There is but one right path: The restoration of democracy in the United States.

Excerpt: *National Guardian*, Jan. 2, 1956

* Amendments:
ARTICLE XIII
Slavery Abolished
1. Neither slavery nor involuntary servitude, except as a punishment for crime whereof the party shall have been duly convicted, shall exist within the United States, or any place subject to their jurisdiction. (Ratified Dec. 18, 1865)

ARTICLE XIV
Citizenship Rights Not to Be Abridged
1. All persons born or naturalized in the United States; and subject to the jurisdiction thereof, are citizens of the United States and of the State wherein they reside. No State shall make or enforce any law which shall abridge the privileges or immunities of citizens of the United States, nor shall any State deprive any

The outstanding fact about the Negro group in America, which has but lately gained notice, is that it is flying apart into opposing economic classes. This was to be expected. But most people, including myself, long assumed that the American Negro, forced into social unity by color caste, would achieve economic unity as a result, and rise as a mass of laborers led by intelligent planning to a higher unity with the laboring classes of the world.

This has not happened. On the contrary, and quite logically, the American Negro is today developing a distinct bourgeoisie bound to and aping American acquisitive society and developing an employing and a laboring class. This division is only in embryo, but it can be sensed.

The Negro Businessman: In the eighteenth century, the Negro slaves and freed men were guided within by Negro religious preachers in church units. Then, in the nineteenth century, they developed leaders in the Abolition movement. After emancipation they had the intelligent leadership of preachers, teachers and artists who, together with philanthropic black men, guided and advised the group.

But from 1910 until after the First World War, Negro businessmen forged to the front and today they form the most powerful class among Negroes and dominate their thought and action. This class bases its ideals on American

person of life, liberty, or property without due process of law, nor deny to any person within its jurisdiction the equal protection of the laws.

(Ratified July 28, 1868)

ARTICLE XV

Equal Rights for White and Colored Citizens

1. The right of the citizens of the United States to vote shall not be denied or abridged by the United States or by any State on account of race, color, or previous condition of servitude.

(Ratified March 30, 1870)

business methods and aims. They spend conspicuously, organize for widespread social enjoyment and extravagance and regard the private profit motive as the end of thought and life.

The three hundred or more Negro newspapers, with few exceptions, are mouthpieces of this bourgeoisie and bow to the dictates of big business which monopolizes newsprint, world news and credit facilities. Franklin Frazier,* a leading American sociologist, once president of the American Sociological Society, has recently emphasized the significance of this development in his *Bourgeoisie Noire*, published in French by the Librairie Plon.

The Negro Worker: Negro public opinion is thus tied to current American thought either by reasons of security or sometimes by direct money bribery, especially during political campaigns. The dream among the intelligentsia of an independent Negro vote, devoted to Negro progress, has therefore largely disappeared except under stress of some particular outrage like the Till** murder.

Opposite the small Negro bourgeoisie is the great mass of black labor. It is at present only vaguely aware of its conflict of interest with the Negro businessman. This businessman employs a considerable number of Negroes and exploits them quite as much and often more than whites because of the limited jobs open to Negroes. As, however, the Negro laborer joins the white unions, he is drawn into the great labor movement and begins to recognize black business exploitation. But the main mass of American labor is at present in conservative unions under reactionaries like Meany.*** So far as these unions

* E. Franklin Frazier: 1894–1962

** Emmett Till: A fourteen-year-old boy wantonly murdered in Mississippi. The racist murderers were tried and freed in 1955.

*** George Meany: President, American Federation of Labor-Congress of Industrial Organizations admit Negroes, the Negroes follow the reactionary philosophy of the white.

Here the black, like the white, is restrained by charges of subversion and fear of loss of jobs.

Excerpt: *National Guardian*, Jan. 23, 1956

MESSAGE TO THE ACCRA CONFERENCE

Africa, ancient Africa, has been called by the world and has lifted up her hands! Africa has no choice between private capitalism and socialism. The whole world, including capitalist countries, is moving toward socialism, inevitably, inexorably. You can choose between blocs of military alliance, you can choose between groups of political union; you cannot choose between socialism and private capitalism because private capitalism is doomed!

But what is socialism? It is a disciplined economy and political organization in which the first duty of a citizen is to serve the state; and the state is not a selected aristocracy, or a group of self-seeking oligarchs who have seized wealth and power. No! The mass of workers with hand and brain are the ones whose collective destiny is the chief object of all effort.

Gradually, every state is coming to this concept of its aim. The great Communist states like the Soviet Union and China have surrendered completely to this idea. The Scandinavian states have yielded partially; Britain has yielded in some respects, France in part, and even the United States once adopted the New Deal, though today American socialism is held at bay by sixty great groups of corporations who control individual capitalists and the trade union leaders.

On the other hand, the African tribe, whence all of you sprung, was communistic in its beginnings. No tribesman was free. All were servants of the tribe of whom the chief was father and voice.

When now, with a certain suddenness, Africa is whirled by the bitter struggle of dying private capitalism into the last great battleground of its death throes, you are being tempted to adopt at least a passing private capitalism as a step to some partial socialism. This would be a grave mistake.

For four hundred years Europe and North Africa have built their civilization and comfort on theft of colored labor and the land and materials which rightfully belong to these colonial peoples.

Those in control today of the dominant exploiting nations are willing to yield more to the demands of the mass of men than were their fathers. But their yielding takes the form of sharing the loot — not of stopping the looting. It takes the form of stopping socialism by force and not of surrendering the fatal mistakes of private capitalism.

Either capital belongs to all or power is denied all.

Here then, my Brothers, you face your great decision: Will you for temporary advantage — for automobiles, refrigerators and Paris gowns — spend your income in paying interest on borrowed funds; or will you sacrifice your present comfort and the chance to shine before your neighbors, in order to educate your children, develop such industry as best serves the great mass of people and make your country strong in ability, self-support and self-defense? Such union of effort for strength calls for sacrifice and self-denial, while the capital offered you at high price by the colonial powers like France, Britain, Holland, Belgium and the U.S.A. will prolong fatal colonial imperialism, from which you have suffered slavery, serfdom and colonialism.

You are not helpless. You are the buyers and to continue existence as sellers of capital, these great nations, former owners of the world, must sell or face bankruptcy. You are not compelled to buy all they offer now. You can wait. You can starve a while longer rather than sell your great heritage for a mess of Western capitalist pottage. You can not only beat down the price of capital as offered by the united and monopolized Western private capitalists, but at last today you can compare their offers with those of socialist countries like the Soviet Union and China, which with infinite sacrifice and pouring out of blood and tears, are at last able to offer weak nations needed capital on better terms than the West.

The supply which socialist nations can at present spare is small as compared with that of the bloated monopolies of the West, but it is large and rapidly growing. Its acceptance involves no bonds which a free Africa may not safely assume. It certainly does not involve slavery and colonial control which the West has demanded and still demands. Today she offers a compromise, but one of which you must beware:

She offers to let some of your smarter and less scrupulous leaders become fellow capitalists with the white exploiters if in turn they induce the nation's masses to pay the awful cost. This has happened in the West Indies and in South America. This may yet happen in the Middle East and Eastern Asia. Strive against it with every fibre of your bodies and souls. A body of local private capitalists, even if they are black, can never free Africa; they will simply sell it into new slavery to old masters overseas.

Awake, awake, put on thy strength, O Zion! Reject the weakness of missionaries who teach neither love nor brotherhood, but chiefly the virtues of private profit from capital, stolen from your land and labor. Africa, awake! Put on the beautiful robes of Pan-African socialism.

Excerpt: *National Guardian*, Dec. 22, 1958

THE AFTER-THOUGHT

Hear my cry, O God the Reader; vouchsafe that this my book fall not stillborn into the world wilderness. Let there spring, Gentle One, from out its leaves vigor of thought and thoughtful deed to reap the harvest wonderful. Let the ears of a guilty people tingle with truth and seventy millions sigh for the righteousness which exalteth nations, in this drear day when human brotherhood is mockery and a snare. Thus in Thy good time may infinite reason turn the tangle straight, and these crooked marks on a fragile leaf be not indeed

THE END

Excerpt: THE SOULS OF BLACK FOLK
(Chicago, A. C. McClurg and Company, 1903)

INDEX